A MORTAL SPRING

A MORTAL SPRING

BY FRANCISCO UMBRAL

TRANSLATED BY HELEN R. LANE

HARCOURT BRACE JOVANOVICH
NEW YORK AND LONDON

Requests for permission to make copies of
any part of the work should be mailed to:
Permissions, Harcourt Brace Jovanovich, Inc.,
757 Third Avenue, New York, N.Y. 10017.

Library of Congress Cataloging in Publication Data

Umbral, Francisco.
A mortal spring.
Translation of Mortal y rosa.
I. Title.
PQ6671.M2M613 1980   863'.64   80-7946
ISBN 0-15-162338-4

Printed in the United States of America

First edition

B C D E

. . . this mortal and pink corporeality
where love invents its infinite.
—PEDRO SALINAS

A MORTAL SPRING

WHEN I wrench myself away from the thicket of dreams, the dark forest of sleep, and retrieve myself, I slowly make myself whole again. For my dreams no longer interest me. To hell with Freud.

Everything we are, I grant, has this reverse dream side, this foundation or this messy pile of rubble underlying it. Some ironic soul might wonder what kind of dreams Kant, Descartes, Hegel, those monsters of reason, had. The total mental repression that their philosophic systems represent was bound to have a chaotic, painful, tormented reverse side. How do we deny the half of existence that lies in shadow, if that is where dreams are located? There is a time in our lives when we decide to be nothing but our dreams, and Surrealism is an age of adolescence insofar as it seeks its sustenance in dreams. There is a maturity, a classicism—that may come at any time in life—when we make a deliberate choice in favor of our reason, our rigor, our human stature. But so what? It is as childish to live on dreams as it is to live on syllogisms. One obviously lives on what one can, and it takes a long time to learn to live on realities, on things, on objects, as natural beings do. Man is a being who lives at a far remove from himself, someone has said. Yes, man is a being of utopias, of distant horizons, of "lyrical projects." Man must learn to be a creature who lives on what lies close at hand, a shepherd of the immediate.

My dreams give me only a hopelessly muddled version of something crystal clear that I possess. When I dream, I am the confused exegete of myself, the amanuensis whose hand-writing is indecipherable, the pedantic bore who insists on noting everything down to the last trivial detail, thus making a mess of the whole business. Dreams offer a gratuitous and obscure commentary on my life, a life that has no secrets yet has a shadow.

On this point I agree with Sartre, who denies that dreams have any meaning and maintains that they are incapable of producing a single coherent image, for the moment that I form a coherent image "I am already awake." My dreams don't interest me, just as my past is of virtually no interest to me anymore. In dreams I make Surrealist poems of the prose of life. André Breton lives in me and comes out at night to devour me bit by bit. To hell with Breton. I know that I consist of sewage, slime, putrefaction, but at this point I find it boring to search for corroboration of that fact, and I am no longer fascinated by my own feces, that infantile fascination that lingers on in the poet, the neurotic, and the psychoanalyst. Only people with no imagination have to resort to their dream life. It is quite apparent that nothing ever happened to Breton or Freud. It is as primitive today to interpret dreams as a revelation of the past as it was in Joseph's day to interpret them as a revelation of the future. The feeble lantern of dreaming does not cast one iota of light on the future, and all that it projects on the past are vague shadows, blurred outlines, and ambiguous versions of what was once perfectly clear. To dream of my dead mother or of furnaces that I was entrusted with turning on and off as a child, and of the thousands of stairs that I climbed, is merely to repeat, in tedious detail, like a bad film whose reels are mixed up, a life that I don't want to remember. It is surrealistic enough that one's mother lies dying while one climbs thousands of stairs running errands. What Surrealism can dreams add to a reality that is already so unreal?

I wrench myself away, then, from the swampy forest of dreams and take up where I left off as best I can, I pick up bits and pieces of reality lying sadly strewn about the room, I bend over at the waist, and my kidneys, carrying their burden of the past and alcohol, groan softly. I am on my feet now.

The first happiness of the day is having escaped the puerile perils of sleep, the conventional terrors of nightmares. Plain ordinary clear-mindedness is better than delirium. One almost always has bad dreams, but what we still have left is the imagination that is indispensable if we are to invent reality in the fashion of Antonio de Machado, though a reality with fewer flies and less filth than that invented by the Arabic-Andalusian poet. My right eye aches, as it does every morning, since the prose read the night before, coagulated and inflamed now, is there inside that eye that labors and suffers and has passed nothing on to my brain; instead an entire book is stuck underneath my eyelid and is pressing on my fifth cranial nerve. Another daily incident: the superb, insistent, gratuitous erection that one has after a certain number of hours in bed. There is no recipient in the whole wide world worthy of such an erection.

This erectile ostentation is directed at nothingness, at a nonexistent woman of shadow and dreams, an insubstantial Becquerian phantom of mist and light. It is potency without desire, the sheer mechanism of sex revealing what I have in common with the piston, the machine, and the anthropoid. If a woman were there before me, the phenomenon would have human dimensions: proper, efficient, reasonable. But this way, it is simply one last unnecessary show of the jungle that inhabits me, a calamitous power of nature, a scandal. We have carefully concealed this mechanism that works all by itself, burying it beneath literature, nuances, alexandrine verses. What is love, when no love could provide as convincing a demonstration as that produced by the pressure of the intestines and the starch against the spinal column?

Fortunately, reality erases the anthropoid in me as the waking state erases dreams. I am no longer Breton or a bare-assed monkey. At the exact midpoint between the two, I am myself, urbane, civilized, reasonable, properly behaved, and discreetly perfumed.

My face in the mirror. My hair not what it once was.

Time puts its threads in your hair, the poet says. Gray hairs, white basting threads at those very places where we're coming unbasted, where we're unraveling, showing how badly we're made, how hastily we were sewn together. I'm losing my hair, and shall continue to lose it. My hair is falling out a little bit at a time, but it is definitely falling out.

When I was a youngster, I used to like to comb my hair in such a way that a rebellious lock fell over my forehead, like the heroes of my childhood, but Grandma used to have my head shaved bare in the torrid heat of summer, and the violet evening breeze filtered in through my naked skull, chilling my imagination. Later on I wore it however I pleased, combed forward, combed back, with sideburns or without, and I played at making a wig out of my own hair, just as men who are bald play at persuading themselves that a toupee is their own hair. Western philosophy—Hegel, Marx, Descartes— is a philosophy with a part straight down the middle, while eastern philosophy is bald, a philosophy with a shaved head. I am not a philosopher, and I have changed hair styles in exactly the same way that I have changed speculative systems and conceptions of the world—in short, whenever I felt like it—but my combs come out as heavily loaded as hayracks at certain seasons, full of hair. It's time to go back to the dermatologist, to don turbans of foaming shampoo that make me look like a fakir, to apply lotions, to rub and massage vigorously. This is all to the good; my hair falls out anyway, but the peripheral irrigation of my brain is thereby accelerated.

One loses the blondness of one's hair as one loses the blondness of one's soul, the golden halo with which life adorned us at the beginning. One's hair hesitates for a while and then eventually decides to be what is, just a plain ordinary mousy brown, the color of those of us who will never get anywhere in this world. Once upon a time my hair was a blond wheat field through which there passed doves as feminine as hands, spring zephyrs, sudden gusts of wind. Today the only thing that passes through it are sad combs—and ideas. Ideas that once carelessly raked through my long hair and left it strewn with metaphors, that nowadays pass through my head and leave it a neatly furrowed, sown field, and that one day will leave it an untended garden once again. For one begins by wanting to create for oneself an irreproachable ideological coiffure, and it takes a long time to arrive at the salutary abandonment of barbering and gardening. The way to live one's life most freely is with a wild garden for a head.

But I still resort to sprays, shampoos, lotions, colognes, and my hair continues to fall out nonetheless. Once upon a time it was the panache of my imagination, but as we begin to have less imagination we begin to have less hair. My forehead is making great inroads into it, as though I were thinking more than I once did, although the truth is I am thinking less. Everything that once nested in my hair—dreams, birds, mouths, skies, fires—passes me by now, winging past far above my head, and it is a rare day when my head seems populated, inhabited, as though some exotic bird had made a nest in it with little wisps of hair and love.

It is frightening to look at oneself in the mirror, to comb one's hair, if only with one's fingers, so that the rare bird of the idea won't fly off. It is time to sit down and write, because the nuthatch is already pecking at my prose the way I peck at my typewriter; the woodpecker is eager to build something, who knows what. But then suddenly, as I am putting a new sheet of paper in the machine or shifting from one paragraph to another, I realize that the bird has flown, that it is no longer there.

Or, to put it another way, I realize that I am sitting alone writing, metamorphosed into a mere typist, that there is no bird here any longer, or that there never has been one. It's pointless to go on pecking at the keys. I cover my typewriter and read what I've written, or I tear it up. And I wait for the bird to come back another time, the bird that is not inspiration, of course, nor the Holy Spirit either, but just what I've said: a bird in flight that is an idea.

❡5

An extraordinary thing that alighted on my forehead the night before, when I poked my head out the window to check the weather, that has slept inside me all through the nightmare, and that in the morning is silent and does not burst into song because it is hoping that I will do so. When I go ahead and sing, it flies away, perhaps because the typewriter has frightened it with its machine-gun calligraphy. Hence one is afraid of being left with no hair and no bird—that will be the time to put a bullet through one's temple, because when life takes the hair from our head it seems to be inviting us to do ourselves in with one good clean shot through our bare skull.

Hair, hair. Hair was a torch gleaming in the lyrical night of my adolescence. A torch that has now gone out, a mere dreary-looking handful of tow in the bright daylight of adult clearsightedness. Tides and eras have passed through my hair. A head of hair is like a sea, a head of hair is an ocean, long locks are flowing water, a river in which the bare hands of a woman will not bathe twice. Hair was music once, and now long hairs fall out of my comb, leaving in the air the strings of a harp that has come unstrung.

One must take care of one's hair. My entire self is turning into a hairkeeper, a keeper of the thinned-out forest of my hair. But it will be gone sooner or later, and I will be forced to live with a bald-pated stranger, ugly-looking and silent.

How did I come by this face? I see a blond, scowling young child in the yellowing lithograph of the past. I see a schoolboy with a white, flat-looking face in that classroom photo—the postwar period, a cold, miserable school, children tattooed by the barbarism of poverty, the globe on its stand in the schoolroom, the schoolyard with its peeling walls. I see a conceited adolescent with hair combed back in a high pompadour and sad eyes. And now I see hair that is rapidly disappearing, defeated eyes, a nose that is growing longer and more bulbous in death's premature greed, a bitter mouth, a pentagonal face, the shadow of a beard, cheekbones high as ever. It is as if life had intended a Chinese child first, then a pale-faced adolescent, and later on, changing its mind, a near-sighted, bitter, ill-natured man. An invisible hand keeps remodeling my face, molding my expression, first drawing and then erasing successive sketches of what I was, what I am, what I will be.

In the end, since death has bad taste, it will keep my worst likeness, the most inane, the most contorted, the maddest, and preserve it forever—although this is only a manner of speaking, since after they bury you life goes on from inside death, and you are peopled with other, lesser lives and evolve toward the elegance of the skeleton or the stickiness of slime, until you have become either a dandy of bone or a toad. It's not true that death puts a stop to everything. It's just that the sketchbook of life closes and your face ceases to be your face, for we are all simply a succession of sketches, and after the very last sketch comes the mask, the skull.

Is there anything more false than a skull? It is our most perfect disguise. Inside the skull is the person looking out at the world, and the skull looks at us with the eyes of a mask, for the skull is not the truth of a face but rather its ultimate mask. "Rose, the dream of no one beneath countless eyelids," Rilke wrote.

What terrifies us about the skull is the discovery that it is also a mask, the mask that nothingness wears, the disguise behind which no one gazes out at us. You can't guess who I am, you can't guess who I am; you don't know, you don't know. And there is no one there to know. The skull has often been used as a mask in carnival processions and in paintings. We wear the truth—the flesh—outside, and the mask inside, as though we were unwilling to show our true faces in the beyond. Every cemetery is a masquerade. The skeleton has the face of a thief, it wears a disguise, and that is why we are so wary of it. The dead are not to be trusted, and skeletons are greatly to be feared.

• • •

For the moment, my face is not skeletonlike, and I try to find in it the child who has passed this way, but I can no longer do so. I search for the dead man I will be, for the man advanced in years who will want to believe that he has earned eternal glory, but I don't see him either. It's useless to ravish destiny, to do violence to the telescopes of time. One sees what one sees and no more. Every so often, when you are least expecting it, you meet yourself as a corpse in the mirrors of a salon, or discover in *grandes dames* how the future will strip you of your flesh, but if you attempt to do so in a deliberate, methodical way, the flesh closes up and smiles, it becomes compact and wholly present. Today has a way of acting in self-defense, so to speak; our body does not know what its tomorrow will be and assumes the attitude of a rose when we try to make it into a metaphysics. The flesh does not permit itself to be turned into literature. Sometimes, if we catch it at a moment when it is distracted, it is transparent and allows bone and nothingness to show through. But if we go about this in a premeditated fashion and steal a glance at our flesh or at that of another person out of the corner of our eye, the ranks close up, the figure becomes a harmonious whole, the colors become a thick impasto. Life is opaque to death. It is this fact that makes it possible for us to live.

The cliché that at a certain age every man becomes responsible for his face is absurd. I am not unhappy with my face. What I didn't like about it at one time I have now accepted, and its very permanence has enhanced its value. Physical features become sacred through repetition. A misshapen nose, a family trait, passes from father to son, crossing the seas of heredity like a little skiff, and is no longer either ugly or attractive. It partakes of the nature of the sacred, for its very repetition, its magic way of reincarnating itself, has rescued it from vulgarity, has ritualized it in the eyes of the family and their intimates. Everything that persists in time gradually becomes perfect.

Age confers nobility on a person, no doubt about it. Every young man is a parvenu of physiology. But this nobility is no consolation. There is nothing like youth. Youth is a divine vulgarity. The passing years stylize us, make us more aristocratic, dignify us somewhat, and make us stand out from the crowd. But we find the glorious democracy of youth preferable to these distinctions, these decorations of age that life pins on us. What we love and seek in the young woman is time, her brief span of days, age at its most miraculous, something universal and anonymous: what we seek is the splendor of the species. It's impossible to find the woman beneath the radiance of her tender years. Then the radiant glow fades and a mature woman appears, a human being, a life. This is less interesting, however, to us great lyrical male egotists. Not because of the sheer sexual drudgery we foresee, but because we have more faith in lyricism than in psychology; we would rather be dazzled than understanding when it's a question of love. A mature woman is a human abyss into which we feel no desire to cast ourselves. The young girl is a whirlwind of light and flesh. I don't know what women may think of this face, my face. In any event the woman, being more civilized, less lyrical where love is concerned, prefers to read a face, prefers a legible face—as mine now is at my age.

My naked white body. Why so white? The down that covers it is a forest blanketed in snow. My grandmother was pleased that I was so white when I was a child. She used to say that my whiteness made up for my ugliness. Grandmothers create these traumas in us, they tell the child these cruel things that accomplish nothing except to destroy the warp and woof of the affective life the child is in the process of weaving. A harsh grandmother with the blood of Castile and León in her veins is more often than not the diametrical opposite of an affective warp and woof.

White, as I say, white as milk, white as a lily, an incurable whiteness. Nowadays people with white skin lie in the sun to tan themselves. Not a good idea: a tan is a garment, a disguise. A woman with very white skin is more naked. Pigment, whether natural or acquired, clothes the body, covers it with yet another garment. Flesh in and of itself is like the soul: it is white.

I am saved by the down on my body. Without it, I would be unbearable, it seems to me. A woman yearns for a little bit of jungle. Nakedness is the jungle that all of us still have within ourselves. The flesh is the ultimate, impossible paradise lost. Nature, a patch of wild forest, must be preserved in the body, because sex is above all a rediscovery of origins, and bodies that have become unnatural through excessive care and artifice have destroyed the wild forest within them. They are worthless.

For the civilized man today it is woman who is a wild forest. And vice versa. Virgin forest, for the body, is another body. The few remaining traces of the lover of the wild that we still possess are the only future we have left. It pains me, as I say, to think that this whiteness will be lost, dissipated in the air of my death. I feel no regret at the thought of losing my arms, my legs, my life, my heart, my genitals, my pituitary. But I regret the thought of losing my whiteness, of ceasing to be white when I cease to be myself. I am more saddened by the prospect of the death of my whiteness than by the prospect of my own death.

Let us pay careful attention to the last natural signs of our body. We are a hieroglyph, a royal codex that civilization is reading. We are now almost entirely deciphered. When the hieroglyph has been deciphered down to the very last detail man will have no future left. Our future is our enigma, the capital we keep eating into. But we necessarily make our way toward the light. That's the way it should be. May humanity be enlightened at last and may I die while still in darkness— die without every last shade of meaning having been brought to light, having been completely deciphered, remain like a codex that goes only halfway, incomplete, fragmented, no more than a hint.

May the whiteness of my skin not be explicit, all too explicit. Ah, the enigmas of what is white. Ah, the obscurities of light!

If the greatest light is the least shadow, the greatest whiteness is the least darkness. Though I am white, I am not a blank. Beware of me. I am what I am. Enigmas of snow, of foam, of clouds. Forms of whiteness, the hidden galleries of a body that seemingly conceals no mysteries.

To take whiteness as truth is to vastly oversimplify things. What is white is neither clear nor simple. What is white is as enigmatic, inexplicable, and immutable as what is black. White and black are absolutes. The nature of green is more bearable—pleasant green, *el verde ameno,* the classic writers said, or the lyricism of blue, the life of red, the movement of yellow. What is unbearable is the absolute, which torments and blinds us. We are not made for the absolute, perhaps for the simple reason that the absolute does not exist; it is a mental abstraction that stifles us.

That is why mystics suffocate.

Einstein discovered that as light expands against the force of gravity it shifts toward red. Red, then, is a tragedy, a degeneration or a transformation. Even symbolically, in ideological symbology, red is synonymous with dialectical transformation, with the struggle against the gravity of history and the world. Red is dynamic. Thus, according to Einstein, white would be the beginning of the process, effortless light, flowing with the current. Is this what my whiteness means? I have resisted such a conclusion, perhaps unwittingly. White as the point of departure. One must pass through all the colors, a fugitive from the rainbow, a pedestrian trudging along the entire length of the spectrum.

In dreams, in love, in the moment of waking, my white, naked body.

• • •

An anthropoid lives in my genitality. It awakens and stretches its limbs each morning with the most joyous of expectations, no doubt supposing that a day fornicating in the forest awaits him. He must gradually be persuaded, by way of lather and alexandrines, that that is not how things will be, because what really awaits him is a day of telephones, trousers, tepid tea, taxicabs, and twilight conversations.

The anthropoid rebels, or used to rebel, but to no avail. He is gradually learning not to fling himself forthwith on young women he happens to find sitting next to him at the movies, at the theater, at concerts, or at the dinner table. From time to time he tries to rape the nice young *gringa* who has fallen asleep in my library, expurgating my books for a master's thesis, or else he severs her jugular vein with the edge of a sheet of India paper, but generally he is quiet and depressed. The anthropoid frightens women at first, or so they pretend at least, though in reality they find the person he inhabits not anthropoidal at all when the moment of truth arrives. Though perpetually in search of occasions to reproduce himself, the anthropoid takes to his heels the minute the occasion presents itself, leaving me alone with the woman, and suddenly I am simply a weary, nearsighted writer.

As I become a bit anthropoidal with the passing years, thanks to the force of inertia of the eternal return, the anthropoid gradually becomes more human, more civilized; he acquires a melancholy, philosophical turn of mind. The day my anthropoid dies I will have turned into a librarian and that will be the end of me. One must take one's anthropoid wherever one goes, the way the animal tamer takes his tiger with him, and let him out regularly for a stroll through life.

The anthropoid gets bored when I read newspapers and begins to cast restless glances about him. He impatiently awaits his chance to fling himself on the neck of some woman. You spend your life trying to train the anthropoid, and when you have him almost tamed, it turns out that it is you yourself, the best of yourself, that is beginning to fail to come up to the mark, to return to the wild, to rebel. There was a time when the anthropoid wanted to be a poet, but he threw away a great many rough drafts of his poems. I was unable to make an amanuensis of him. He then abandoned his spiritual activities for good and has spent his days trying to get back to the forest, sniffing the call of the jungle. The hand of the anthropoid is the same one that wrote Shakespeare's sonnets, for some do a better job of domesticating their anthropoid. All of culture is a circus act, in the sense that it involves taming a wild beast, educating an animal, humanizing a monkey. The anthropoid often betrays me by way of my nose, and it is of no avail to be sitting aseptically reading or writing, for the anthropoid makes generous use of my pituitary and smells women everywhere. We fear the anthropoid, it is true, but what we fear most, when it comes right down to it, is that he'll die on us.

I have taught him many things: to read Nietzsche—who wasn't a bad anthropoid himself—and Juan Ramón Jiménez, to enjoy Proust and recite Quevedo, but I haven't managed to make him like music. In the last analysis, literature and painting—he also likes painting—are arts of the wild, thickets of words and colors, but music, despite the fact that Nietzsche found it so dionysiac, is a stylization of no one knows quite what, and the anthropoid doesn't go for stylizations.

He has proper table manners, though not always, and he can transform a copulation into a poem, a masturbation into an essay, and a cry into a smile. It saddens me now to see him so well behaved, so prim and proper, so resigned. The melancholy of the adult male is the melancholy of a tamer. It is what an animal tamer must feel, if he is at all sensitive, when he has managed to subjugate the old tiger, to domesticate the noble lion. Women come in search of the anthropoid, though

《 13

they do not say so, and it is only a perversion of culture that has made them prefer the anthropoid who can cite verses, passages from the classics, and the titles of books. A man always remains something of a trained monkey in the company of a woman if he knows things, because women bring out the monkey in one, and once the monkey is on stage, the best thing to do is to allow him to behave like one.

What makes a man feel insecure in a woman's company is that her mere presence arouses the anthropoid, and he understands that everything he says and does as a writer, as a man, as an intellectual, as a friend, as an urbane city-dweller, will always be slightly artificial, fake, circuslike, because the anthropoid is there on stage and simply reciting his role or ours. "But this anthropoid is playing the part very well. One could easily take him for an academician," is the one thought secretly running through women's minds. Because they too are unable to keep themselves from seeing the anthropoid and watching his every move, even though they come round in all good faith looking for the writer, the friend, the stranger. Any situation between a man and a woman is tense and false, because there is always a third party between them, an anthropoid who comes and goes, who gets impatient and interrupts things every so often to say: "Well then, are we going to begin or aren't we?"

Only when the man realizes what little there remains in him of the anthropoid can the man and the woman again see each other as urbane creatures who have left the sheltering forest behind, living helplessly within culture, expelled from paradise, with all the fruits of the tree of knowledge turned into books. We feel more comfortable now, but sadder, filled with melancholy. Latinists call it the *tristitia post coitum*. The real truth of the matter is that the anthropoid has departed.

Hands, my hands, one hand darker and the other lighter, as though one of my grandfathers had been a marquis, the other a metalworker. Our hands are still cast in the mold of

Cain; they retain the structure of the hand of the anthropoid, of the first man, of the last hominid, the hand that robs and kills. Hence there are no innocent hands. White hands that offend no one. Perhaps they are the most offensive. My right hand is more highly developed, it has lived more, it has a longer biography, so to speak. My left hand is more feminine, more sensitive, it alights and then takes wing again. Hands: Mary and Martha.

There is no equality in life. Discrimination is part and parcel of our being. One hand is always more aristocratic than the other. And the other hand is more of a toiler, more violent, more long-suffering. How do we overcome this discrepancy? We must arrive at a world where everyone is ambidextrous. Laborers work with both hands, they have brought about peace and reconciliation between their hands, perhaps the best and greatest peace that man can achieve within himself. The intellectual, the bureaucrat, the man who writes, the man who speaks, has one hand that is public, active, hard-working, and the other hand—usually the left one—is as if dead, encased in a shroud of whiteness, mummified, at rest. This is indicative of the imbalance in our lives, the unevenness of our souls.

When we were children, hands were like claws that every so often our mothers washed, scrubbed, clipped, filed, so as to give them back their hand nature, their humanness. We have had periods when we took good care of our hands and periods when we totally neglected them. A hand becomes a thief all by itself, or makes itself into a fist. We follow our hand's lead as it drags us after it, seeking to fulfill its destiny.

The hand has written graceful alexandrines, miraculous musical scores, but its shape has come from violence, hunting prey, criminal deeds. It is the hand of a primate that has gone in for elegant penmanship. It is not so much culture as war that has shaped it. Our hand is a tool and a weapon. It bears the imprint of violence. For that reason, when it writes laws, they are usually violent, and when it writes poems they are usually lies. We have blood-stained hands; man's hands have done a great deal of killing. War and crime are simply the act of washing our hands once again in the primordial blood of prehistoric destructions, in the warm red throat of our slaughtered brother or the sacrificial lamb.

He who works with his hands, who makes his living with his hands, is more faithful to the structure and the destiny of the hand. I who have reduced my hands' activity to pecking away at a typewriter, to gesturing during a conversation, to discovering the secret of caresses, have atrophied hands. We often speak of someone as having "the hands of a pianist." The jungle claw has contrived to draw the bowstrings of music taut, and hands are little by little passing from light to shadow, or from shadow to light, from the jungle to the salon, from hunting to culture, from the crime to the poem. We have built the whole of culture with a murderer's hands. A hand has more fingers than it needs to hold a pen, and man has more hands than he needs.

Hands play their part in love. They are important. Hands have a code; they speak in the act of love, and act. Hands are birds and feet are stones in the act of love. It is very easy for a hand to become a claw on the body of a woman. It is better to go to the woman with the hands of a pianist than with the hands of a thief so that the woman will not feel sacked and plundered, but tempered, played with a light touch, finely tuned.

Women's hands fascinate us, hands masculine, vigorous, autonomous, or the hands of a child, of a nymph, schoolgirl hands that smell of the classroom. A woman's dark hands, with fingernails gleaming like jewels. The lyrical fake jewelry of fingernails.

Nothing reveals our body, invents it, creates it, better than a woman's hands. The incurable tendency of the man to cast himself in the role of the protagonist has made a cliché and a myth out of the man's hand possessing the woman's body. But the woman too has the knowledge, the ability, and the desire to unmask the man, to shape him with her hands. A woman's hands show me the measure of my life, the true dimensions of my chest, the reality of my body, the contours of my mind. A man's body remains a nebula until the hands of a woman shape it, mold it, define it, make it concrete. His body floats and a woman's hands anchor it in reality. In the same way, I too can create a being with my hands, with my caresses. She was not aware of herself until I caressed her. The mythical, biblical, generative act of manual creation of life by God, the master potter, is continually repeated (or takes on its only historical reality, from which the myth was born) when one being creates another being with his or her hands, when a man creates a woman or a woman a man.

The sleeper wakes, the clay becomes a person. From out of the mire of a life merely lived from day to day, I make a different being, "desired and desiring," dawn; with my hands I model the form of her desire. In love, hands are creative. We envy the man who truly creates with his intellectualized hands in love, in sex, in contact. The murderer's hand becomes a liberating hand when a body slowly turns and awakens beneath it. The hand, an axe, a weapon, a hook, my hand, has days when it is a dove, days when it is the hand of God, and days when it is a claw, which are days when I hide it, when I hide both my hands and wash them a great deal, in order to remove every trace of the blood of I know not what crime in the remote past or the future of the species.

The skull. But what about the skeleton, the other bones, that figure made of calcium and phosphate that inhabits me, that hard, ugly individual that constitutes me? Bone, down to which love never penetrates, the poet said. Nothing penetrates to the bone. Neither love, nor beauty, nor thought, nor emotion. Only blows go down to the bone. To the marrow that burns gloriously. Inside the bone, the marrow is like the soul of bone, the electric cable sheathed in calcium. We are construction work, a job to be done in the cosmos. We are inlaid with tiles, and varnished like a painting by an old master or a modern floor. When I look at myself (one must take the body rather than the soul as the point of departure for reflection), I realize that masons, milling-machine operators, painters, electricians, and carpenters have worked on me.

I can still follow the traces left by the joyous work crew who made me. Expert electricians in blue overalls finished all the wiring in my brain. Cabinetmakers carved my feet with their fine chisels. Craftsmen skilled in the use of clamps made my fingernails, and specialists in ornamental plasterwork molded my bones with a most delicate touch. We are an inspired construction job.

Divine handiwork, the mystic or the lyric poet would say. This is going too far. It is not a question of dressing God up in workman's overalls, but of realizing that the oldest, most noble, most humble occupations have their model and origin in nature itself, and that man, if he is not the measure of all things, is at least a scale model of the universe designed with the very best of intentions.

Let us speak of the skeleton, of my skeleton, which is the one I know best, yet even so I really don't know it at all since the skeleton is the great stranger. "The dead man that I shall be is amazed to be alive," a French poet writes. "What a vocation to be a dead man my skeleton has," a Spanish poet intuits. While philosophers have always spoken to us of the soul, poets have preferred to speak of the body, and hence have come closer to the truth.

The soul is the mad dove flying through the skeleton, flitting from one limb to the other, pursued by metaphysical sodomites. "I love a tree more than a man," Beethoven wrote. I for my part love a body more than a soul. The soul is a diadem we never see, whereas one's body is oneself. Coequal with the body is the skeleton, which lives its own life and is not dead: far from it. I know what my body likes, but I have no idea what my skeleton likes. I wish I knew so that I could give it pleasure from time to time.

Is it a sports fan, is it an intellectual, does it desire the skeletons of adolescent girls, does it like to read or play blindman's buff? We know little about the body, but we know nothing about the skeleton. Since the routine medical X-ray was invented, the skeleton has learned to pose, and we leave the clinic reassured in the knowledge that we have a skeleton, an armature, something solid inside. The body is awakened by kisses and caresses. But only blows and hard knocks awaken the skeleton, thus causing us to suspect that though our body is a hedonist, an epicurian, a bit of a pantheist (a mutilated pagan, E. M. Cioran would say), understanding, tolerant, down to earth, and a pacifist, our skeleton is undoubtedly a most uncongenial fellow, an ascetic, a hermit, a loner, a contemplative, a mystic deaf and blind to temptations, who spends his days muttering the prayers that we neglect to say.

When you take a bad tumble or give yourself a hard knock you realize that you have an inhuman rigidity inside you, and the most disconcerting thing is not the bruises, but the sudden realization that you are so hard, so inflexible, so physiologically obstinate. We human beings are not a unity, not even a political unity, because the tolerant flesh has an intransigent skeleton inside it, a dyed-in-wool conservative standing at attention at all times, stiff as a ramrod.

As an attempt at a first rough sketch of skeletal psychology, we might point out that what characterizes the skeleton is its refusal to let its arm be twisted, its stubbornness, its intolerance. Admittedly it bends here or there, because it obeys the same laws of mechanics as a locomotive piston, but don't ask it to bend anywhere else, because it will break.

The skeleton is an ancestor that we carry inside us, and when we see an X-ray of our skeleton we are struck by how closely it resembles Grandfather, since all we remember of Grandfather is his mortal remains being reinterred, moved to their final resting place: there was nothing left to rebury but bones. We carry our ancestor not only in our soul but also in our bodies. This ancestor gets bored, while at the same time he is ashamed of our fornications. He would actually like to go to war, since that's the whole point of his being so hard, so rigid. The skeleton always has an active military air about it, and we have turned it into a retired army man who drinks coffee, lounges about on sofas, reads books, and fritters away his time with women.

Only contortionists have managed to cultivate their skeleton, but the result is obviously a primitive culture that does not go beyond the circus ring.

Pitigrilli says that elegance depends on one's skeleton. Quite true. It is a clothes horse, so to speak, for the flesh. This is its most noble function, and its one faintly redeeming feature. My flesh will melt away and the skeleton, the ancestor, will remain, the one that I no longer am. Flesh is present reality; bone is eternity. What is eternity? Calcium phosphate. Then after a time the bones too disintegrate or are lost. The ancestor, who was a neat and orderly sort, cannot bear the thought of losing a bone. But I am happy at the thought.

My little boy is here, glowing with his own golden inner light, alive, despite all the cats of death staring at him from the corners, making things speak, delighted by the talkativeness of objects and corners, peeking through the back of life, seeing the reverse side of everything, discovering the world's musical tops, its jack-in-the-box springs. My little boy, his short life, his golden hair, with no time behind or before him, a tiny creature in danger, as perishable and improbable as an apple bobbing in the sea, only just arrived here after that birthing late one afternoon, when I saw myself mirrored in his plaintive cry as he hung head-downward.

Early infancy, that period in our life that we lose forever, that we never know anything about, is given back to us only through a son; it is lived all over again with him. As I looked at those closed eyes, that rose-colored tearful cry, I saw myself on the other side of time—the baby, his feeble courage, his pink ferocity, his total faith in life, without past or future, an absolute present, and the way he has gradually cleared a path for himself through language, the way he has parted the fronds, acquiring words, and has now reached me, emerging from the thicket that separated us, from the forest of names and letters, and is now on this side, an inhabitant of the alphabet.

We never lead a child by the hand. He always leads us, takes us where he is going. The child takes us to the kingdom of what is small, he hastens to our own childhood that lies fast asleep, he puts us on the most direct path, traveled only by the ant, the tiny olive pit, the solitary snail, the rolling stone.

Walking down the street, through the fields with him, he gives us the measure of our exile, for he belongs to skies that journey to the light of day, to the sudden sharp report of the hour, and we no longer do. We have placed ourselves at a distance, through thought, reflection, impatience, order. The child, who has no plans or projects or programs, immediately becomes one with the changing seasons, forms part of meteorology, is natural within nature, and everything smiles upon him.

There is no point in trying to become like one of these little creatures, even if we are moved to do so not out of an ardent desire for moral purity, but out of a desire to be an integral part of nature. An impossible endeavor that, because the child, I feel, is the measure of my exile, and my son has been born of me in order to live everything that I can no longer live myself: changes in the weather, sun and shadow, garbage heaps, and the myriad tiny things that clutter the open countryside. How long he ponders what is simple, how quickly he understands the unexpected. Cruelty and tenderness are one and the same thing in him. He rips the world to pieces because he loves it, and his tiny footsteps gradually take possession of the planet, lovingly and lightly, for though the earth scarcely feels the weight of a child, he is more a part of the earth than we are, in that we have long since become travelers journeying through the conventional spaces of reflection and fear. He takes in everything as if it had been there waiting for him all the time, and he can look dogs and cats straight in the eye, something we never do. The child passes from sleep to waking without a word, without a break, without the least trauma, and goes about the house rousing everything that had been sound asleep until he came along: doorknobs, the locks of closets and cupboards, the bottoms of all sorts of receptacles, the other side of objects.

There is a dimension of a house that only a child discovers. If a giant adult, a stranger, takes him in his arms, the only thing that interests him is a single button on the stranger's overcoat. At the seashore all his interest is focused on one shell. He knows how to reduce what is vast to his own measure, how to shrink the entire world to his own size and come to terms with what is immense by way of what is small.

At night, he enters the realm of dreams as if it were a living cave. Any position suits him, and sleep always overtakes him just as he is about to do something, his hand stretches out to tug at light by its tunic or seize water by its throat. I touch his hair that is light itself, his face that looks simple to the eye but reveals a multitude of details to the finger tips, his skin with the texture of cheese that loves so many things, his flesh that smells of the street, of cold, of furious living in the present, and I do not allow myself to feel the pain of my awareness that this child of mine was born and thus may die. I want to feel only this chunk of existence, this violent outburst of animality that has stolen bits and pieces of language from man, this sudden outcropping of humanity that peeks into the dank caves of other species and converses with them.

A child partakes of the nature of fruit, cats, and man. He is a cross, half apple and half feline. He is eager to live, but he does not know that he is already inside life, that currents running down through the centuries have culminated and halted their course in him, that the present dwells within him. Every so often, I see him not as a son but as a miraculous harvest, as a momentary creation of time. All the forces of life pass through him, and this same material that has become a child might well have become a tiger, a fruit tree, or a little brook. The conjoining of days and electrical currents, of energies and seeds, that has brought forth a child might equally well have been unleashed to produce a twilight, a harvest, an electrical discharge, a puma.

What my finger tips touch in the child are beautiful heterogeneous forces that are inexplicably harmonized. He appears to owe his life more to the workings of chance than to a deliberate plan. And since he still is an integral part of the universal currents that have constituted him, he immediately recognizes the brotherhood of nutshells and fruit rinds, fish and slime. He is flesh in its wild state that the teeth of the patient combs of language have gently penetrated.

IT is Sunday and people have disappeared inside the church. On a morning such as this, as mankind entered into conversation with God, the poet had a talk with his donkey. I walk along the street, holding my son by the hand. I talk with my son, as in his eyes there appears a donkey's innocence and stubbornness.

Everything is outside. There is nothing inside. It is a morning of outward manifestations. What the world *is* is right here in front of us. The secrets of the universe, its childish, ultimate keys, quiver in the pure morning air. Primary truths wag their tails in nets of light and sky. Altars of sun, deities of rock, empty successive firmaments, fresh expanses that humanity has left abandoned, shutting itself up inside the church. My son and I stroll through streets that lead straight to the blue sea of the sky. We have met no one as we have walked along. Not even God. The little boy picks things up off the ground, comes face to face with a passing shrew mouse, follows a dog's wagging tail as though it were the secret oscillation of the universe. Dogs and my son, creatures without God, pure beings that sniff around, visitors of every nook and cranny.

Holding my little boy by the hand, I venture farther into the depths of the morning, the depths of the day that conceal no mystery, the free and easy slowness of the hour. We stroll back and forth. The churches are hemmed in by a ring of silence. We feel very much at home, the child and I, in an empty world, in the deserted outlying districts of heaven. We are able to walk north on suburban grass, triangles of wretchedness, the sorry, dirty fringes of the mountains that are at once near and far.

• • •

No implacable presences threaten us, no Sunday gods keep a watchful eye on us, there is nothing between the world and ourselves. No one's magnificence casts a shadow over the mountains, no one darkens the snow, the sun, the day. Nothing looks down upon us from anywhere, and everything sees us without casting its gaze upon us. We are a man and a child in the world. The child is whole, compact, his span of years brief and transitory, seriously threatened, with the biography of a fruit and the cultural attainments of a bird. I am confused, vague, fuzzy-minded, but the morning air clears my head, attunes me, simplifies me, strengthens me. The child sets out to discover things, and I to rediscover them. The dogs stare at us and perhaps see us as dogs.

We see the kiosk with its gleaming brass, toys, seeds, humble anise flowers, pathetic chocolate artillery. The steam rises from the food that is being cooked, fried, roasted, stewed, painfully transformed. For the child this kiosk is culture, the whole of culture, the compressed bundle of every possibility, dream, war, story, speed, laughter. The kiosk is the child's Universal History. All of my Universal History, culture, war, science, everything that has ever been written and thought, is reduced for me to a stand where seeds, toys, newspapers, and magazines are sold. In the immense morning, the little kiosk of culture, the complete arsenal of wars and philosophy. The child goes off clutching roots, weapons, dried fruits, objects, things, realities in his hands. I go off with newspapers and periodicals, nothing but words, words, words—printed matter, small type, the thread of slime left by the human snail, repetition and occlusion.

We are on the way home now. People are returning from church, families clustering together like coral reefs, a lingering happiness between them, a sun of tradition and the flock. Not one of them has grasped anything, yet they all pool their share of nothing and create something. Sanctified, they scatter to pastry shops, stores, stands, and, their appetites whetted, they pass from devotion and half-shadow to the airiness of kitchens, from the nothingness of the tomb to the full light of day. They die for half an hour, they exercise their skeletons, they rise to their feet, sit down, kneel, speak in silence, yet strain all the while to be dead people that speak, dead people that sit or kneel, the better to show their devotion. And now, unwittingly, they allow themselves to be caught up by reality. Their lives await them at the church door, and they hastily immerse themselves in the day, unconsciously fleeing the deep hole that had them trapped. They fill the street.

The morning has lost its vastness. My little boy is no longer the only youngster around. We are still strolling about, and the four cardinal points touch us, but the miracle has ended—the miracle that the rest sought inside four walls, in the shadow, and that we found outdoors, in the open air, in the streets.

The others turn their backs on life, face the wall of tombs, and, having held in the breath of life for a time, they plunge into the light with pleasure. Instead of engaging in these spiritual gymnastics, the two of us have wandered through the streets, like dogs. Our time is not shrouded in veils of darkness. We are a man and a child who venture naturally out onto the steepest slopes of light.

Broken fingernails, chipped nail polish, peaks of reddish-purple lacquer on the pale fingernails with threadlike ridges. I must do my nails, the flat, jagged fingernails, with lots of soap and baking soda, and the pink or mauve or magenta or violet polish—never again that blood-red one of the day of the fiesta, that he didn't like a bit—and the swollen finger tips, dark red, a dirty, blackish pink. So five finger tips, five fingernails, live on each hand, the nail polish cracked, dry bark that has peeled off. Getting there in time, finishing the dishes, the sweeping, the washing, getting there in time to catch the bus, getting there in time and going into town, the same every week.

The plates with hunting parties painted on the borders, the cups with greenery around the rim, the decorated dinner service, the porcelain with hunting scenes and shepherds tending flocks, the broken dishes—you're bound to break a dish or two—the glasses with little gold rims, also chipped here and there, like the girl's fingernails, like the nail polish. She is sitting down now, quietly, not moving, stolid, pensive. Doing dishes, sweeping, washing, cleaning. But motionless now, her thick hair pulled back tautly, her eyes soft with sleep, a fleshy nose, a large, resigned mouth, still a little like a child's. Feet wound about each other, enjoying the rest, hands folded, or pausing on her skirt, or embracing her own body, her percale shoulders. Large, heavy, broad hands, with fingernails painted mauve, pink, red-violet, and the polish chipped and cracked in capricious, geometrical patterns. Getting to the bus on time.

Hairy forearms. A tall girl, mannish in a quiet, gentle way, adolescent, silent. The heat of a kitchen, the stubborn dripping of a faucet not completely turned off, an atmosphere of sweeping. Washing dishes, sweeping, scrubbing, cleaning. She is now sitting motionless on the stool, lace edging on her sleeve, halfway up her arm. Lace edging with pointed tips bent back, with wrinkled points, with points like tiny dirty balls, and here and there a stretch of clean white lace, neatly ironed, impeccable. Submerged in the health of her body, she becomes one with the heat of the kitchen. She is not aware of her body. Her body is lost, asleep, scattered about, gathered together again in a shapeless heap in her lap. The hands, solid, hard, heavy, stand out in strong relief in this vagueness. Her hands. She moves them slightly, contemplates the darkened knuckles, the first, second, and third phalanx, and recalls these strange names, these funny words, from school, the town, her childhood.

She contemplates her broken fingernails, five hard jagged petals, the pale, rigid fingernails, the white flesh underneath, pink on the other side, pink on the finger-tip side, the blunt finger tip, soft in some places, hard in others, insensitive in certain spots. Washing clothes, doing the dishes, cleaning the rug, sweeping the hall. She is quiet now, her body asleep, though perhaps awake in the depths, that itching sensation crouching down there, that desire, that errant restlessness. He said he didn't like painted fingernails. I must do my nails. Get there in time to catch the bus to the town, the same every week. The bus is waiting, its ancient engine idling.

The plates with scenes painted on the borders, the soup tureen like an all-day hunt, the cups and the bowls showing separate scenes in the great overall hunt. The big soup tureen is the apotheosis of venery, the summing up of everything that has been happening on each cup, each plate, each bowl. There's not a single cup you haven't chipped, daughter. A little triangle comes off the edge of a plate, of a cup, so easily. It's like a tooth suddenly falling out. Why is it my fault, then? The dance in town, taking care of Mama, Papa's clothes, washing your father's clothes, the heat, dry, harsh heat. The body's pink vagueness is slowly awakening. The broken fingernails—I must do my nails—the chipped polish, the mauve-colored fingernails, an unpleasant, no longer gay, hard color.

Looking again at a deep flesh, the secret wound, the underwater breathing of the sexes, the sad greed whereby my genital mouth becomes dehumanized, becomes vaginized in the stinking dialogue with this blind wound that has also become a mouth in its turn, in a revolting way, addressing me in slime-words, hair-silences, blood-smiles. An aura of the slaughterhouse and erectile secrets that give me once again, for a moment, the obscure, acrid, wounded paragraph that a woman's body is.

I come from the green, monstrous, musical northwest. I come from vast stretches of water and cloudy skies reaching to infinity, from green hours hovering motionless above the woodlands, from ever-changing itineraries through the world, from corners of light, of water, of time glimpsed along the way, from perfect little spheres, bright and quiet, in which one takes eternal rest.

Lives nicely rounded off, congealed in a single glance. It is the landscape that travels. A fisherman, a woman along a road, a child in the mud. An entire life seen in an instant. The hills pass by like music, the woods sing like choral societies, the skies journey like estuaries. But if we stop, if I step down onto the ground, the world is immense, still, solemn. We pass from one time to another time. Eternity slows down enormously. There is no longer music or choirs or journeying. Only the dark perpetuity of a sky devoured by the towering forests and the raw mountains. I am no longer the fleeting lord and master of lives and landed estates; I disappear: I am the tired gaze of a city-dweller that cannot catch in its frail net the immense fish of the world wildly flapping its tail.

The sea: changing its gender, sometimes *la mar,* sometimes *el mar.* To return. I would like to have been one of those little lives, a complete life within the confines of a cottage, a boat, a pond. But I do not belong to this. Here nature, dreamed of so often from afar, so often read about, gives me only the measure of my solitude. It is the size of what I am not. I can write all about it, but literature is the ultimate distance that we perpetuate between ourselves and things. (Literature, alas, is no longer what it once was for me, a way of possessing the world and fornicating with it,

❡ 30

but rather a way of secularizing my isolation.) Ponds, skies, lives, rains, seas, mountains, woodlands where I was never free and never will be. I take a deep breath and the world transfixes me.

Then to my sorrow it withdraws from me.

I am listening to my son grow.

THE heraldic white horse presided over everything, its whiteness and its power duly established in that confusion of buffoons, breeches, duennas, saints, virgins, gold and green musicians, red and yellow devils, wild-eyed gray-bearded prophets in fits of ecstasy, gleaming blue gods. The horse was there, making its way through the uproar of the Renaissance, trampling the long gowns underfoot, illuminating the shadows of sin, at once ennobling and bestializing that entire harmonious and chaotic, solemn, street-roaming assembly of clerics and great ladies, captains of heaven, and archangels of clay.

A child spectator, a wonder-struck child, I saw it all from inside my red-and-white robe. Dressed as a deluxe choirboy, I saw myself as an extension of the painting, yet another of the figures living their Renaissance fiesta, pagan and Catholic, in the great parish sacristy, between heaven and earth, between the smaller cupola of that nave, a shipyard for holy clouds, and the floor inlaid with great black-and-white tile slabs. The giltwork, the candelabra, the cressets, the remains of altars and the ruin of Virgins peopled the sacristy with a disorder and beauty that were like the chaotic state of what in the great painting was harmonized, whole, young, thundering. My long red-and-white choirboy's robe allowed me to enter the enormous painting on the wings of its ample skirt, to reach the side of that horse of living plaster, of sculpted flour, of white and silver. In the half-light of the sacristy I contemplated with the eyes of a new and awestruck spectator the completeness of a world around me that was nothing but ruins, a memory, a repair job, nothing.

The reality around me was also made up of golden visitors' books and magnificent vessels, but it was as if everything were now defeated by time and covered by the patina of a past that in the painting became color and a living present. The wide-eyed child did not know who painted it. Indeed, it never occurred to him that someone had painted it; rather, he took it to be a fascinating reality, a sort of film at once magical and true to life. It was as if he were seeing at the same time the brilliant past of things totally present, and their wretched present altogether past.

A spectator without limits or limitations, I was caught up by the painting's whirlwind of goddesses, men, and women. I was the only one to enjoy the descent into reality of all the figures, their act of taking possession of the sacristy, the church, and the world, their movement with the rhythm of colors and the swiftness of music. Even if I knew the name of the artist, I wouldn't tell you, for if I did we would return to limits, to distances, to art as spectacle, contemplation, erudition, catalogue, and we would lose that wild and untamed magic faculty, at once childlike and eternal, of participating in art as if it were another, more harmonious life, warm, real, and promising.

In winter, when the church was freezing cold, they made the great sacristy into a church and one could spend the entire mass gazing at the painting. What was lost in worship, liturgy, heaven, and salvation was gained in art, history, earth, human and divine. Never again has that choirboy looked at a painting or experienced a painting in the same way as in those days. In the big church, in the real church, was Gregorio Hernández's sculpture of *Christ Lying at the Foot of the Cross,* a body of great splendor and reality, with hard tears and carved feet, but that Christ did not become human to me until the night my grandfather had a bad attack of bronchitis and the women of the household stripped him and put cupping glasses on his great ancient chest, that like the Christ's had a hairy pelt growing out of it. Like Christ he too had a wound in his side, he too had trouble breathing in his niche, he too looked around with the whites of his eyes turned up, which is how dead men look at things, seeing under the eyelids a realm that is neither heaven nor earth.

Dark rooming houses, fake-leather armchairs in the parlor, plastic flowers, pentagonal mirrors with a clover engraved in each corner, the redolence from the kitchen, rickety tables, and pages of the week's newspapers hanging on a nail in the toilet, carefully cut into even-sized sheets, thus forming a new paper, an unusual daily that the editor-in-chief could never have foreseen, that one could leaf through as one contracted one's bowels, gazed at one's hard, angular knees, or at the edge of one's shoes—these shoes have had it. Through the little window high up on the wall that looked out over a labyrinth of yards full of spider webs, cats, and rooftops there came the noise of the city, the surge of cars, a tiny print of blue sky—here at least we never lack for blue sky, which is a joy and a blessing from God—music blaring out of radios, and the didactic, pedantic language of television sets. One must win the struggle for life, the literary duel, or cry out in horror, à la Baudelaire, before succumbing.

The man who ran the rooming house, a lazy bachelor, was in the kitchen, doing the crossword puzzle, feeding the canary, shuffling off to piss once in a while, talking on the phone to the grocery store. And the women who helped around the establishment, his sisters, also unmarried, talkative little things with flowered smocks over their black sweaters, bustled back and forth doing all the work. In one room there was a consumptive pianist who played in an Afro-Cuban nightclub, in another was an ex-seminarian, reading Saint Augustine and masturbating, and in another room was I, with an aching belly or an aching heart, mentally writing the book we write all our lives without actually writing it, from the womb onward, with our neurons, the book we will still be writing when death catches up with us.

I don't know whether one found in them the farewell to lost youth or the portrait of the perverted young man or the chronicle of life lived in anger, but in rooming houses the truth of the capital, the miserable soul of the city was to be found, like a dense precipitate, that bottom layer consisting of toilets, pyorrhea, nicotine, oratory, and concubinage that politics and literature have in common. Because you had come to that, to sinking down into the warm slime of life, to breathing in the halitosis of the great masters, to living in a milieu that resembled a decayed molar and experiencing everything that appeared in the newspapers, turning yourself inside out and dumping out everywhere the entire sack of printed words that you'd been carrying around in your kidneys all your life.

Or else those rooming houses with a standing wardrobe in each room, where you rented a single room. Rooming houses are the political, literary, and theatrical hotbeds of the city. Those who wrote the history of the country penned their works in the stuffy rooming houses in the center of the city, and only the wall of their adjoining rooms separated the rightist historian from the leftist historian. Those who years later voted together in the Royal Academy or in Parliament were old friends who had once lived in the same rooming house, shared the same toilet, and still bear in their hearts the same burning resentment of foul coffee and cruel strumpets, an indelible imprint on their youth.

Let us say that the mid-century mark had already been passed and the mirror in the rooming house reflected a blurred image of a young man, blurred as the photograph of him taken that morning in January in the schoolyard. And he saw in the mirror his glasses with lenses that weren't thick enough, his hair combed back in a flat pompadour, his sensitive mouth, his faded suit, his tired tie, and tears, childish tears, the last tears and the last trembling of an intellectual black poplar tree whipped in the spring wind of the future.

• • •

Beds that had been prized possessions of good families, gilded Baroque-style beds where the best couples of the district had slept and begat, beds that were not prostituted, like the daughters of a notary, by the goings and comings of transient lodgers, beds rented out one night to the foreigner from the movie industry and the next to the man come to the big city from the provinces. Beds with a history, where one slept badly, or all too well, feeling like the firstborn of a great family, waking up in the morning beneath a canopy and an ornamental plaster ceiling—ironically, since the immediate task at hand was to take to the streets in search of a job and earn a few pesetas.

You were the intruder in a life, the usurper of a bourgeois privacy and intimacy that changes of fortune had turned into a rooming house, and you moved amid rococo furniture and delicate colonnades, and you slept in a huge family bed, made up with the sheets and comforters that the widowed landlady supplied to her lodgers. Those sheets were still so cold from dead men that they sent chills running up our spines rather than a feeling of warmth and intimacy, and yet before venturing out into the freezing hall in our bare feet in the morning, we would have liked to prolong the illusion for a few moments, to turn our self-delusion into the truth. We would have liked, in short, to be the lazy scions of a bourgeois dynasty.

Or the plain, unadorned beds of the deceased in other rooming houses, the narrow lumpy cots with what felt like straw-stuffed quilts, barracks cots that were better training for life, beds so lumpy and saggy and rickety that they drove us out into the street. Never a bed all our own, never our private, intimate possession.

The sex organ, that soft, gentle thing that moaned when we were children, that inside of a flower that could just barely sing, that little vegetable secret that gradually leafed out in luxuriant fronds of pleasure, urgencies of pain, that contrived to proliferate, to burst into flame, to burn like a clandestine spring or summer. The sex organ, shy plant that moaned with love in protest against the austere lines of type in the catechism books, against the severity of families and the legion of sins.

Key of time, sigh of the flesh that one day would be all of the flesh, tiny rivulet of life in which later all of life would be drowned. They didn't tell us that it had to be washed, cared for, handled, stripped of its leaves. They told us, rather, that it was secret, not to be talked about once it lost its original childhood grace, its amoeba's innocence, and began to grow more aggressive and full of fire. And so we scraped away its scales with our fingernails, in the cold postwar schoolhouse, and it was the great urinary power that could warm our hands, travel clear across the street, and scare girls.

It began to torture itself, to desire itself, a rapist of wool coats and pinafores, a fornicator of canvas virgins, damsels on the walls of toilets, lusty matrons modeled out of empty air. At a certain point it seems as if life is going one way and one's sex organ another. It takes some time to learn that one's sex organ is the way, that there is only one way. An unseen tree of desire and proliferation was sprouting in our souls, and a shameful deposit of saltpeter burned our clothes, and from there one goes on to the sex organ as aggression, as exhibition, this being another way of putting up with it. How difficult it is and how long it takes to come to terms with one's sex organ, its truth, its plenitude, to allow it its peaceful, pleasant invasion of one's life, to accept it.

It was not an enemy that you bore within your flesh, nor a secret, nor an evil. It was the dammed-up spring that you would have to turn into a serene, free-flowing one. But you were not taught this. So it passed, secretly, by way of dark women, veiled bodies, hands of blood, by way of the trembling flowering of sicknesses and the eucharistic percale of sweethearts. It would be a long time before it gently navigated waters tinged with pink, a woman's time, the silence of an entire afternoon. It would be a long time before it became the violent flower of inner springtimes, but today it is master of itself, full of memories, with pelts, sets of teeth, nights, bloodshed, nymphs, and reptiles as its heroic trophies. It has created its biography, it has backstitched the world's seams, it has lost its importance as a weapon and its shyness as a plant, and it is now flourishing, in ripe, full flower, luxuriant and lyrical in the half-shadow of the future.

What security, what peace, what virile silence emanates from it, so that all of one's sexuality becomes soul. To fight against it is to scourge it, to hem it in, to enrage it. Sex must overflow the banks of the flesh. It is the Nile that we bear within our soul, and when it has placidly bathed the world it leaves us serene, secure, and luminous. The sex organ is a flower or a monster. One can choose to carry around either a hidden monster or a flower standing proud and tall. Almost everyone chooses the monster, hides it, punishes it, feeds it, or kills it.

But the sex organ, which is meant to be a flower, suffers if it is turned into a monster. Something is going to grow on our body. A rosebush or a reptile. The choice is ours. We have been taught that it is a reptile. Why not let it be a rosebush?

People live with their reptile, with their filthy sewer, and it shows in their eyes, in their faces. A rosebush that is ashamed of itself soon turns into bristling thorns. Let there be light for rosebushes. A bright lily, a happy orchid might well come forth and take a stroll through life, but instead a nest of vipers creeps furtively about. Guilt, evil, that terror-stricken literary heritage that has been ours since time immemorial. Life is too good or too bad. We haven't yet learned that life is gratuitous. When we have learned that life is gratuitous we will lose our fear of sex.

It doesn't cost anything because it isn't good for anything. There is no need to pay for it in blood, to render it its due out of fear. We must simply lend ourselves to it and allow it to go on as it pleases. Sex is the coin in which we have decided to pay for life and to get back what it owes us. Renouncing sex, mortifying it, making it guilt-ridden, is our way of paying for life with sex. Using sex, exhausting it, harrying it, is the way we make life pay us off in sex. We will never learn that life is sex, that sex is not coin, that it is not a matter of loan-swapping, but of allowing the spring waters of life to flow freely and color the world. Sex is the most precious thing we have, it is our own self, and that is why we want to tame it, to make it into something that will buy something: immortality, forgiveness, life itself. But sex, which is my self, which is life, suffers when it is fragmented. I look at my sex organ, now freed of its mercantile, metaphysical, negotiable status. I look at my sex organ, that is no longer a coin, no longer a weapon, that seeks to buy neither life nor death, nor to do violence, but simply to illuminate the world, to illuminate me, to cast bright beams within feminine shadow, to bring light to light and darkness to the night.

It does not know that history conspires against it. It shines there in the flesh, in all its innocence, in its natural state of grace, an embolus or a tiger.

But the eyes, my eyes, the eyes that I look at myself with and that look at me in the mirror, the eyes through which I see the world, through which the world appears to me, brown eyes, slightly slanted once, tired eyes today, looking smaller behind glasses than they are, the left one weaker but better at making out fine detail and putting what is small into clear focus, the anthill of letters in a book, for instance, the right eye more active and aggressive, more weary and bloodshot, all the world's culture having painfully passed through it and remained stuck inside it, its dulled, blunted edge causing a burning sensation. I baste the world together with my eyes.

Eyes imagine when they read, see what they create

through the act of reading, give plastic precision to concepts, to thoughts. My eyes graze in a book, and sometimes when I close the book my eyes remain inside eating fresh leaves, and I go through life blind, without eyes, without seeing the world, because my eyes are still looking at what they have read, because they have buried themselves in type. When I am master of my eyes, I look at the world and landscapes come before them in a whirlwind. When one is conscious of one's eyes, it is as if the sea were looking at the world. Eyes are the most aquatic trace of our origins in water, and when a man looks at terra firma, mountains, he is still a creature from the sea, and it is this sea creature that contemplates the mortal dryness of the planet.

A woman always lives in my eyes. Looking is the only form of total possession. Seeing a woman breathe, seeing her move harmoniously, holding her prisoner in one's retina, in one's pupil, without her knowing it. The body of an unknown woman falls within the orbit of one's eye and lives in it, painlessly, gently inhabiting it. Looking at a woman.

The sense of touch is blind, the sense of smell rushes along at a gallop. Mouths are frenetic. Ears are dull and slow. The eye alone takes in totality. Reconstructing a woman from her voice, from her touch, from her taste, from her smell—that is imagination. Imagination is the flight of one sense by way of all the others. Imagination is synesthesia, the sense of smell seeking to be the sense of touch, the sense of touch seeking to be sight. Imagination is born of a limitation. Sight is less imaginative, perhaps, because it possesses more. But sight needs to imagine what it sees, to round out and color the woman's body, to bring what is far away closer, to place what is close at a distance. Looking is not enough. One must internalize what is outside and see it inside.

Looking at other eyes is frightening. Eyes burn eyes. The ancients spoke of the evil eye. And what is the evil eye but the eye of evil? Eyes are refreshed when they look at the world and get burned when they look at other eyes. Nothing sets us on fire the way a look does. A look of hatred, a look of love, a questioning look. I know that my eyes can set the world on fire. I know that other eyes can set me on fire. Only other eyes. A woman's eyes. Eyes are swords. Raised swords. In love, eyes are lakes that flow into each other, lakes whose waters are decanted from one to the other. A man's eyes and a woman's. In life we attack and we bleed with our eyes, through our eyes. The phosphorus of eyes, a gaze of phosphorus, the bright gleam of eyes in the darkness of the body, eyes like rivers in the dryness of the body. Fish, that is what eyes are, navigating through the light or navigating my body. The aggressiveness of eyes! Eyes, a blank weapon.

Learning to look at eyes, to look slowly, deeply, learning to listen with one's eyes. No one can bear the interrogation that silence subjects us to, someone has written. No one can bear the interrogation that eyes subject us to. Eyes strip us bare and eyes conceal us. How long it takes for a man to become the master of his eyes, how long it took me to inhabit my eyes, to live in them, to people them. Because ordinarily we flee the region of the eyes, finding it too brightly lighted, and hide ourselves in the cellars of the body. One must make up one's mind to live in one's eyes, as if they were the skylight, the bright dormer windows on the top floor of a house, looking out on the body's skies. Being in my eyes so that I may be seen, so that I may see. Setting up residence in my eyes as if in the body's sunniest rooms.

My eyes, which have seen the world, take their repose in the flesh of a woman, an unknown woman. In sun, in shadow, close at hand or far away, that woman's body whose solidity my eyes deduce, those limbs that must be contemplated until they lose their coherence, their meaning, their conventionality—like an often-repeated word—and become only a free form, a gratuitous volume, the pulp of life, solidified existence, involuntary matter, food for the eye. Disillusioned with what is profound, I reside in my eyes.

Summer has come and my little boy has been taken to other suns, to other summers, to groves of shadow in which I lose him, his life as always in great danger, beaches ranting in their dotage, waters that welcome him in their great white beard, in their old age as full of sound and fury as an eternity.

My boy, my son, a perishable fruit, an apple in the sea, an instantaneous miracle, doubly impossible, I am here, in the disorder of your absence, amid the colors, animals, objects, weapons, wheels, and beings of your world, so dead without you, playthings of a lonely sun that scarcely touches them, and your absence looks at me from all the walls, you are incarnated in photographs when I make flattering overtures to the touch of nothingness. But you are not here.

If someday you were not here at all, my son, what would it be like, what would the world be like, the whole of it an abandoned playroom, an empty childhood planet, the universe reduced to the absence of a child? I come and go now, with my adult's hustle and bustle, amid the calm silence of all your activity. I stumble over things you have left strewn about on the floor, I unwittingly destroy with my feet a part of your interrupted game, and the dark surface of your slate looks at me, but to pick up a piece of chalk and write a letter of the alphabet or draw a wolf on it would be to invoke you, to set the world quaking, and I do not dare do so.

How quiet the house is without you, how motherly the house is, a dark uterus remembering you. Your absence has left a portrait of itself in an order that is a disorder, and the flashbulb of other summers fixes on the walls your very brief biography of teddy bears, beaches, disguises, seas, and breakfasts.

The fiercest lions, the birds with the most metallic screech, speak in your soft voice. Your secret bond with the wild fills the pictures of savage beasts in magazines with tenderness, and I am violently assailed by memories of you when an animal passes my way, appears on a page, or has its name spelled out in print. That's enough. When we are children, animals are signs, a leopard stands for a letter and a giraffe for a word. The language needed to communicate with you is animals, and I am pleased to speak this language so that you may understand me and I may understand you. No condescending clown act, no moral lessons, no diminutives. You are innocent, because you have not yet formulated a single idea and you reason by way of objects, you express yourself through the intermediary of wild ducks and friendly wolves. A conventional fauna that we have coined for you and for me. When a dog appears in the street, I am reminded of what is doglike in you, my son, of how much you have in common with an animal, with an errant, vagabond creature. There is nothing like the kinship of children with animals, that secret child with cat's eyes, that rosy-pink wild beast of your body.

I am here, passing through the absence of a child, taking the pulse of solitude, and I feel like a melancholy giant in the tiny world that he has left behind. The sadness of giants steals over me at the feet of what is small, and I want that little boy back home, winding up the owl clock and all the things that cast a thousand sidelong glances at him, look at him, and go tick-tock. The world goes tick-tock when a child plays. The universe is a tick-tock of light and dark. I am afraid now to touch the fragile, abandoned disorder of your games, my son, and I leave them undisturbed, as I leave untouched the sacred workings of chance in your life.

THE sense of smell, odors, that complex world that comes and goes, everything that I have enjoyed thanks to my pituitary, my understanding of the world as odor. Though my eyes are weary, my sense of touch deadened, my sense of taste satiated, my sense of hearing dulled, my sense of smell is becoming keener and keener, for one sense replaces all the others, interprets them, poeticizes them, and I can now speak of the smell of a woman's hair drying in the sun.

Smelling is a poetic activity. Once, when I was a serious young writer, I tried to describe situations, places, in minute detail, but then I realized that describing one smell or one color is much more useful to the reader. Pió Baroja described a street as being long and smelling of bread. That says it all. A long smell of bread. Why add anything else?

Descriptive art, the art of piling up minute details, is immature and boring. Expressive art, expressionist art, isolates certain features and thereby becomes not only more bare but also more effective, for art is reducing objects to a single feature, enriching the universe by impoverishing it, making it less literal in order to enhance its powers of suggestion.

The smell of my son, the smell of children, a delicate fragrance mingled with street smells. The smell of a book, the smell of each book, that swarm of typographical bees that dizzies us and fascinates us when we bury our nose in it. The smell of a woman, each one with her own particular fragrance. Living beings have an aura, their odor. A person's odor cannot be possessed, it is the fragrance of a personality, and that is why we find it so disturbing and so disquieting.

Becoming addicted to smells. Nothing stimulates me more to write than a new, pleasing, suggestive, piquant smell.

Schiller sniffed an apple to put himself in the proper frame of mind to write, they say. Another writer pored over the civil code. Wasn't smelling it what he was really doing?

Literature and painting are dizzying because they have an odor. The vinegary smell of the ink of our childhood days. The wild, pungent aroma of books. The fresh, concentrated perfume of painting, the fragrance of colors, that should be looked at with one's eyes closed. What is missing in the paintings hung in museums? Intimacy, immediacy, authenticity? No, it is smell. Old paint no longer gives off any odor, and painting thereby loses a dimension, for painting has three dimensions, the third being the olfactory. Music has no odor. That may be why I don't respond to it. Smell and taste, the two senses so closely allied, are the most intimate keys to life. To look is to externalize. One must see without looking. One must smell. The sense of smell is the soul's sense of sight.

I am writing this book in summer, with occasional escapes to the seashore, with joyous plunges into nature. Summer is lyrical because time is vaster then; it is "the season complete in itself," and the long days that it brings are like a happy portent of eternity, surrounding us with a suggestion of its glory. Summer is the one faithful copy of paradise lost. Paradise lost exists not in space but in time, obeying the law of the eternal return of the seasons. Summer is duration. Summertime is a reasonable eternity.

Each summer, with the return to nature—even if it is a timid, simulated return—old myths take on new life. In the beginning, the sea was the sea, entirely given over to the innocent play of its colors. Then, with the advent of culture, we began to furnish it with references that had nothing to do with its real nature, that were reflections, rather, of personal fervors. Time passes, erudition fades away, our creative fever subsides, and nature becomes nature once again, as at the beginning of life—simply a deep, clean, transparent vessel, without myths or interpretations. It is difficult to rescue nature from culture. Only the contemplative soul succeeds in doing so. But how difficult contemplation is! Poets and hunters have divided nature between them. The poet debases it with his metaphors, and the hunter humiliates it with his physical exertion. Neither a creator nor a seeker of game, the person who is purely and simply a contemplator is the only one who lives in nature, the only one in whom nature lives.

Having reached the point of saturation with culture, my own and that of others, I find that I am at a beginning and not an end. Cured of literary allusions, I find the world opening itself to me, solitary, vast, harmonious, coarse, and crude.

There is no resurrection of the flesh save summer. All theologies are created in the likeness of the calendar. We have no other reference point. Weather and its changes are the only universal biography possible. As the years go by, one turns from books to meteorology. I exiled myself from culture at the right time. Like all exiles, I dream of the day when I shall return. But it's a good thing to put off returning for a bit. I am writing this book in summer, in the full light of day, but it must also be exposed to other seasons, because a book must be a chunk of time, a concentration of life. The pivot of the book, the tiny pivot, my son, will bear the entire weight of the turning of time and words around him.

Why not a novel? The novel is a bourgeois compromise, monsieur. The novel is the fruit of winter, of stuffy rooms, pipe-smoking writers, and hour upon hour of painful toil. The book, my book, like the summer, must have all the doors and windows open wide, and a flurry of activity outside in the street.

And none of the punctilious recording of every change of mood that the intimate journal implies, either—that bureaucracy of feeling to which certain writers fall prey, filling their insides with row upon row of desks. No. Successive concentric illuminations, a wheel of instants, working the present over, as the bullfighter works the bull over with the *muleta,* until it is exhausted.

¶ 46

Reaching, if possible—by passing through tunnels—another summer.

At times I collapse on my own breast, I grow dizzy from the battle of roots raging in my torso; flames and branches are locked in combat within me, a silent and eternal struggle. My breast, into which the sharp-edged steel weapons of time are now sinking, like fine roots, my breast on which women have slept wide awake, listening to my insides that are a tree, sounding my depth that is a live trunk, or the dark green waters of my blood.

A breast to which my son comes with his little light head, a propeller of words and hair, to mumble a story or tell a dream. I place my hand on my breast and make friends with myself. In summer my breast becomes a ship's prow with seas of sky breaking over it, in winter it closes up, turns in upon itself, and I forget it. I sometimes collapse on my own breast, the map of my life, and moan.

The breadth of a man, the freedom of a body, the hospitality of my breast that has grown with years, a well turned upside-down at the bottom of which there sings a heart that once regulated watches and now collects little pebbles. A chest that is still strong, still erect, that awaits death as timber awaits it, ignoring it. I have a presentiment of its decline, the falling of its leaves, the terrified flight of the birds that nest in it, and in my eyes is the gleam of axes that will fell it in the woodland of the future. My chest, which in my adolescence was frail, has grown broader, and the little lizards of days scamper through its moss, and sometimes a woman's hand, or a mouth, fall on it, as on an old, warm flagstone, and leave the weight of a flower on what there is of me that resembles a tomb.

I end at my feet, thus bringing this minutely detailed inventory to an end too, feet that have traveled such a long way, that climbed dark stairs till darkness fell, the feet of a wayfaring, errand-running, message-delivering child, climbing ever upward, up and up, night after night, by way of scaffoldings, dust left by woodborers, steps, shadows, skylights, the endless stairways that my childhood trudged up, as relatives died, mothers coughed, life snowed, and books flowered in my ignorance. Slender feet now, the feet of a pianist—why don't we speak of the feet of a pianist as we speak of the hands of a pianist, the way I once wrote about hands and now write about feet? Ivory, paths, the paleness and weariness of my feet, the turning wheel that takes me on and on; there is a writer in my hands, but an unpublished, original writer slumbers in my feet. Why not write with one's feet, like those paralytics whose photographs appear in magazines?

The hand has killed, it is corrupted and exhausted. The foot is virginal and idle, and could write with greater purity, originality, and silence. If only ideas could pass through the entire body, arriving at the foot enriched and enhanced, full of subtle nuances. The result would be a different kind of prose, with a different style, a different rhythm, slower and more down to earth. Yes, the feet of a pianist, for pianists have feet too and use them, and music is something that calls for the use of a pedal, like bicycling, a fact that should have made us entertain certain suspicions regarding Johann Sebastian Bach.

To say it one more time. To write it one more time. Health is a delicate balance between conflagrations. Our heads buzz, our eyes hurt, our ears ring, our throats are sore, our bellies ache, emphysemas, vertigoes, insomnia, fear, tooth decay, fibrosis, arrhythmias, coughs. It is a miracle that we are alive. The scientific thing to do would be to die immediately.

The house, my house, an empty space that has run aground, the codfishing boat that we have chosen to dwell in forever. You live in houses, you furnish them, but something tells you that they are not your houses. You go in and out of them. Then one day you find the house, your house, the one that was waiting for you all along, the one that immediately weaves its silence, its shadows, its dust, its time about you, the one you will never leave, the one you will always return to. The house that is beginning to close in like a tomb around you. How compact the house becomes, a beached ship, a stranded caravel, a phantom vessel in northern seas, bearing ever northward amid cold and shadow. The house, the walls, the paintings, my photographs, books, the hum of the refrigerator, the sacred ice of the home, the motor of life, the polar propeller of the frozen boat, fabrics of habit, windowpanes of the day, pottery of the past, wooden beams of constancy. The house voyages, it is restless, one day its bow heads into living suns and another day into dark and desolate sky-seas. Where is the house going, where is it taking us, this house moving elsewhere as we sleep, swept along by what currents far beneath the surface? It lives in us, it feeds on our presence, it makes its walls thicker, sculpts its beds, speaks to us with its tongues of fire in the fireplace, reckons time for us in clocks. It is the towering hold of a vessel voyaging through the sky, and we are the mysterious crew, the stokers of this astral submarine, but only now and again, because it grows bigger every day, closes up, becomes more like ourselves, a flower of cement and music in which we live, sipping death, but then it nods its head like a plant or pitches like a boat.

Books, how books increase and multiply in the house, how those first books from my mother that have accompanied me through countless rooming houses, travels, nights, years, have proliferated. I can scarcely see them now amid the headland of books, the book-lined main wall, a solid wall of print that has changed the structure of the house, and that mortar that makes the pages of certain books we never reread stick together. Books breathe, like flowers, and little by little they kill us, they make the air too dry for us to breathe. But I take care of them nonetheless, arrange them, rearrange them, and they increase and multiply. I forget what order they are in, but they shuffle themselves around and return to their logical geometry of a library, and I know, without wanting to know, where each and every one is, because as we go through life we gradually stop being poets and begin turning into librarians.

Taking a book down from a shelf is like taking a brick out of a wall. The whole thing may come tumbling down and crush us to death. We take shelter from the windstorms of life behind a wall of print, a paper cell in which we become cloistered monks of our own heterodox religions. I can open a book and find myself inside it, because one is merely a bookmark placed between the pages of the novel of one's own life, or I can look at my own books and forget them, books that I have written, rectangles of ignorance and obstinacy, cigar boxes that have no cigars in them.

The flood tide of books, their silence in the night, their smell of library paste and memory, that substance compounded of cellulose and gold that surrounds my life and circumscribes it. How to escape books? They are the brickwork of my soul. In order not to see them, in order not to hear them, I open a book and read.

Peeling an orange, removing the world's skin, stripping the wrappings from the breast of an adolescent mummy. I eat an orange and have an orange-colored day. To be precise, an orange devours me from within. It needs me in order to turn into something else, to survive, and it is already hanging, an orange once again, at the end of time, on the golden tree of my life.

Every depredation is a redemption. Every act of cannibalism is an assumption. I am going to eat another orange. The orange has lighted up my insides like a sun in sections, and the pink-and-white *s* of its peel is lying over there. What a compact, saucy little buttock of the world I caress in the orange. Its taste, its smell, its chemistry are distributed throughout my entire body, and I learn more about life, about the world, about time, from the orange than from all the books of Kant and Plato. I now have an orange-colored lantern within me, and centuries of experience, wisdom, decantation, liqueurs, metaphysical sugars, and lyrical summers that were packed inside the orange, that made it possible. Eating an orange, stripping the wrappings from the golden Egyptian breast of an adolescent girl. If one must believe in something, I for my part believe in the orange.

SOMETIMES I remain for a while inside public toilets, or washrooms as they're called in certain places. One must linger in a familiar or unfamiliar john, in the bathroom of the house or in the public lavatory of a cafeteria, in the vertical coffin of the toilet stall, until the word *toilet* dissolves in the air. Tiled walls, with three tiles missing here and there, three little squares of lime and plaster, wall and time, allowing the rough construction work to show through, three hollow places with a natural symmetry owed to sheer chance, Klee and Mondrian sitting on the toilet seat, one or the other incarnated in me, gazing at the pattern of the little squares, searching for more hollow places, more little squares that have fallen off, the faulty, gray, organic geometry of the wall, in a climate of buttocks, urine, silence, and noise. And the drains, the pipes that gulp water down from time to time, like a sleeping reptile breathing or digesting, the mouthful of black water that slides down the throat of the plumbing. And outside the distant roar of the city. Then suddenly one experiences pure bliss as one realizes that there is not a sound to be heard, that the city is dying away, that it no longer exists, though perhaps the noise from the bar lingers on, the commotion at the counter, or the conversation of two customers, just outside the stall, pissing out their uric acid, let's see if we can get something to eat, I hope you're not as hungry as I am, and here I am, sitting on the john, or standing up, looking at the dirty light bulb, the roll of toilet paper, so uninteresting, so obliging, so mistreated, a stopcock down close to the floor that doesn't open or close anything, the dust and the door.

On the door are graffiti, cracks, names, scribblings with ballpoint pens, brown stains, little burns, cruelties, the trail left by the entire tribe of defecators that has passed this way. A primitive sexuality, crude drawings of genitals that appear to have been traced by genitals themselves, a few political allusions, some vague and others quite specific, a woman's name, Petri, with an oversize *P*: the fellow who wrote it began with an enthusiasm, a grandeur, that soon petered out, for the remaining letters are no more than an indifferent scrawl. What a short-lived thing love is.

Or perhaps he had more urgent business to attend to. Petri. Someone tried to finish the job by carving another name into the door with a pocketknife, but he too got bored and went off after merely tracing the letters with the tip of the blade. One is tempted to steal these toilet-stall doors, these reliefs. How exquisite they are, a perfect example of the decadent taste for what is plebeian, spontaneous, enigmatic, the art that is fashionable these days. Everyone is playing at imitating the element of sheer chance in life, and it is enough to have been clever enough to see the art that life creates, the emotion inherent in people's sense of time, as something made up of discrete bits and pieces, to want to make off with the door, to put it on your back and carry it away, to cart it off through the streets, like a carpenter or an anthropologist. If you put a signature on it it might sell for a great deal of money in an art gallery, but all of that has remained outside, culture, life, my life, the only thing here is a real door, an agglomeration of reality, artificial, synthetic plywood that separates me from the world, isolates me, buries me, that defines my solitude, establishes an individuality that I don't have, divides time, as meanwhile the world outside disappears, sending my way only smells of food cooking, of distance, of noon, of people. I can pull the chain and unleash a rush of falling waters, a noisy cataract, a water-tank catastrophe that will carry everything away and send the reality of the present cascading down on me once again.

Every morning I write, I sit down at my typewriter, I allow dark liquids, luminosities of the night to well up in me, and the entire torrent of language passes through something, someone, because despite what most people think, writing is passive, receptive, just as reading is active, creative, willed.

Merely a question of a trance. Modern linguists tell us that we do not speak a language; rather, language speaks through us. It is the river of language that begins to flow when I sit down at my typewriter. The world expresses itself through me. We are masters only of those sensations that we don't try to rationalize. Let the current of things carry me along, let the universal language speak through me. I can try to master it, to order it, to modify it. Then I will have constructed something, I will have worked, I will have dissected the world and words. One must make oneself transparent—transparency, Lord, transparency, the poet prayed—so that as the world passes through one it takes on the form of speech. When the Surrealists experimented with automatic writing, all they did was deliberately provoke the one thing that makes writing possible. Inspiration. It is certain that there is such a thing as inspiration. Only it is not something external, that ray of light that descends from heaven in mystical paintings, that moon nymph that hovers about profane poets. Inspiration is absolute openness, transparency, hitting upon the right way of making oneself invisible as an intermediary between the written word and the world. There are days when one climbs out of bed feeling transparent, and the best way to take advantage of such days is to write.

If there is no transparency, there is no writing. The toil of an amanuensis may be visible, but that is all. The writer must choose between being transparent or being a pen pusher. Almost all of them choose to be pen pushers, because they have a will to power and because this seems to be a better way of making their light shine before men. Writing is a magic trick in that it is a disappearing act. There are times when the magician isn't at his best; he feels opaque, and remains glued to the spot, unable to make himself vanish in thin air. The writer must allow the light of the world to play over the sheet of paper before him, sunlight to sweep across the words he writes. Almost all writers obstruct their work in progress, standing in its light, casting the shadow of their shadowy selves on their prose.

Prose is prose because it has a shadow, the shadow of the person standing in its light. If it has no shadows it is poetry. That a person achieves recognition for what he writes is another matter entirely. He thereby enters the ranks of professional writers, becomes part of the cultural scene. And style? Style is the modulation that language takes on as it passes through us, like the curve that water assumes inside a jug. Above all, don't cast a shadow. If you don't feel transparent, don't write. Go shopping and bring presents home to your wife. The world becomes a language in you, in me. Making shadows is worse than making rough drafts. The world describes itself, like a teletype machine clacking away. All one need do is drop by every once in a while and tear off the copy coming out.

I write for the pleasure of disappearing. That is my form of transparency. At one time or another all of us have wished to be invisible. Ecstasy, levitation. The world and writing send reflections, flashes of light back and forth between them, and I am in the middle, between two fires, invisible, weightless. To write is to absent oneself. To write is to lose weight. To get thin all of a sudden. How unbearable are the 160 pounds or so that I weigh.

At night, when the world shrinks to the circle of light shed by the lamp, and everything else is incognito, spread out in circles of darkness and nothingness, of stars and factories, I open a book and read, trapped in the light. What am I doing with a book in my hand? What is a book? A rectangular object, a traversable box, a succession of signs arranged in a monotonous order. A book is merely the score of the aria that the reader is to sing. There is nothing in the book, I am the one who projects everything into it. To read is to create.

It is reading, not writing, that is active, creative. From these signs, from this swarm of barren printed characters, my imagination erects a world, a leafy grove, an idea, and birds fly out from between the pages of the book. Nighttime is a bad musician who keeps tuning and untuning his instrument. My son is sleeping nearby, breathing an air of his own, a world of his own, sleeping as though in the belly of the whale of night, swallowed down whole and sheltered, waiting to be returned by way of the whale's mouth, safe and sound, to the cold waters of morning. I read. I open the book and docile worlds appear before my eyes; a man, the thinker, the prose writer begins to work for me, to set up his loom, to weave his fabric of ideas, of words. The spectacle of his toil is always behind what he produces. It is difficult for me to read without being constantly aware of the worker who is laying stylistic bricks before my eyes. Just as I disappear when I write, so does the person who is in plain sight before me when I read.

Perhaps that is what literature is. To disappear in the writing and reappear, bathed in glory, on being read. That is why the effort of thinking involved in writing must not be too obvious. In order not to disturb the resurrection of the flesh that glorifies the author when he is read. Every text one reads has at least two layers. There is a surface of prose, of ideas, and underneath it, like a figure frozen solid inside a block of ice, is the author.

What is exciting, perhaps, about reading is not the content but the possibility of witnessing the unique spectacle of a man working, creating with words his closely woven wickerwork, moving his lantern, making a light for himself that is swallowed up in shadow in one direction when he aims its beam in another. People stop to watch laborers working in the street. The reader too is something of a curious onlooker. I have stopped to watch a man working. He is laying a foundation of ideas, he is erecting an adobe wall of words. The more skeptical we are about what we read, the more transparent the author's toil becomes; we see the man better.

We no longer believe his abstractions. His ideas become less precise, his words lose their color, and the resulting transparency or weakness of the prose allows us to contemplate the person at work behind it. What matters in a book—and what constitutes its most moral aspect—is the spectacle of the workman, his exemplary industriousness, his goings and comings in the workshop of words: his lapses, his omissions, his steps backward, his levitations. There is a man who has tried to create his own vision of the truth and communicate it to us. There is a man who needs to assert himself by changing the world, who needs to explain the world to himself in order to explain himself to himself. There is a man who lives and dies in his book, a victim of shipwreck in the very seas that he himself has created.

Why does one write a book? Out of vanity, out of insecurity, for pleasure, out of blind creative passion, out of love of the truth, which is always one's very own vision of the truth. Out of love of beauty, which also—alas—is always one's very own vision of beauty, the beauty that one is capable of seeing. The sight of a man making anything, no matter what, is always exciting: a book or a barrel, a screw or a furrow.

On reaching a certain age, the reader grows weary and his place is taken by the curious bystander, who above all else wants to watch somebody working.

Walking in the night, peering up at the sky, with my back to the city, I see north winds and stars coming my way. Yes, with my back turned to the city. The city is a morning coat full of moth holes, a cup of anguish, a glove in the mud. I gave the city my first eyes, my heart of wind. I was the adolescent violinist pouring out his music in the streets when all the doors had long since closed and everyone was sleeping or fornicating. Now, with my back to the gleaming dismembered skeleton of the city, I have in my possession the root of each star, nights like a scattered deck of cards, a little boy's slumber, submissive bodies, a book that I glued together this afternoon because the pages were falling out, and all the silence that the countryside sends my way.

The outskirts of heaven, the solitude of a grown man, but no longer purity, the ideal, the essential attained, poetry. That was adolescent lyricism. With my back to everything, poet of my golden years, the fallen dimension of the world, anxieties about my son, my lifework heading nowhere, sex, fear.

Nothing freed of impurity, nothing glorious. Only a parochial peace, and that's quite enough now. Only the passage of death, one tiny step at a time, through life, the retreat to the quiet of this neighborhood, a minor paradise with stars on high, blind airplanes, watered flowerpots, and the slow, soft, quiet dripping of the sky down onto the earth. A single fat raindrop of time, of night, of silence, always just about to fall. An unhurried imminence. When that drop falls, it will be daylight.

Nymphs with their fickle eyes and their mouths of water, nymphs passing by, borne by a current forever flowing in the opposite direction from my life, the nymph of each morning, with her tender young smile, the nymph of each afternoon, all by herself, serious, tough, with her boyish nonchalance and her feminine beauty to come. Nymphs, the obsession of your life; light curves in them, the day sings in the adolescent flax of their hair. Nymphs that have passed through your life, nymphs whose lives you have passed through, the lyrical young girl with her aura of a schoolchild, the blond flame that set time on fire for me forever.

O those older women who were your mistresses, still willing to share their sadness with you, to give you their fidelity, a perfume of domesticity, pathetic duplicities, your frequent visits to them, the habit of them, making love to them in

garrets high up under the eaves with the stench of the courtyard below, on adulterous afternoons, the weekly melancholy
of their bodies, the loneliness of their rooms, so clotted with
disillusionment, always within a net of mended stockings,
and the old words that came out of their mouths. Old mistresses, so faithful, garments with a woman's sweat that grows
cold in one's memory and has a smell all its own.

Remember Serena, write her name, push away the mirror
in which she lived, the green climate of her body, the golden
light she brought in the afternoon, the harmony of an am-
phora, a powerful, lonely love, her mouth like a mask of
tragedy and the precise gestures of her hands, paper flowers,
books, guerrilla fighters on the walls, movies in her eyes, and
the wild, deep moan that you finally managed to kindle in
her faithful, golden flesh.

How many times, lying in bed after making love, at that
hour in the late afternoon when a woman has ceased to be
herself and is moving about the house like a hulking shadow
or a sound, I think, I meditate, I don't exist and I don't
meditate, I wait, I don't wait, I hear children singing in the
street, children who have always been old, the child I once
was, children of late afternoon in the city, sad amid the
lights, the sounds of a densely populated neighborhood, and
that fine line that the world turns into once desire has gone,
once the tension has been broken, once the soaring flight has
ended in a sudden fall.

The woman, I don't know what woman, a bundle of
life, had a body alight with bonfires that I gradually extinguished, like scrub brush aflame that burns itself out, and
now, in darkness or invisible, she is wandering off into the
farthest depths of the house, of the afternoon, as I lie on this
cold bed not existing, levitating in the peace, the emptiness,
the silence, the lucidity that follows coitus. It is a moment

of supreme openness, of profound lack of attachment, of clear light, and love would be worth it if only for this one reason, for having enabled me to reach this gate of shadow where nothing anchors me, this state—the only possible beatitude— of nondesire, of nonbeing, of nonexistence. Plans, the rattle of sabers, all that is there, at a distance, crouching, waiting for me to get to my feet so as to invade me and run me through with weapons, but now, as I slow my life down and abandon my body, I scarcely exist, and the afternoon, like water that is in no hurry, comes to fill up the hollows of myself that I gradually leave behind me.

I want only this, to listen to the children, to be the one who spies on their sporadic last-minute games, and know that an old woman is entering a shop with tired lights and slumbering vegetables to ask for half a kilo of something or other. Ah, that peace of late afternoon, when everyone has unbelted his weapons and the world finally begins to play the slow music of its axes, and we are able to hear, if only at intervals, the sky's sound-and-light show and the breathing of the sick. I stretch out the instant, I am between the immensity of the sky and the body of a waiting woman whose fires have been quenched. For a woman love dies out slowly. She tends it carefully within herself, she humors it, she stanches its flow. As for me, love leaves a great hollow in me, a marvelous accessibility, it leaves my breast open and my eyes immense, and the entire world hurries to fill me, to pass through the crystal into which I have simplified myself without breaking it or staining it.

What an hour of silence, so often experienced in my life, on those humble occasions when the high tide of afternoon overtakes me as I lie in bed, shipwrecked by sickness or sex, and rocked in its cradle. The poem writes itself within me by itself, but only when I was a dull-witted child did I want to write it down. How to believe in nothing? There is merely a little peace, a rendezvous of stars, in this violet-colored truce of nightfall, before bodies turn into bulky, loosely tied sacks, before hearts turn into stones lying on the bottom of sleep. Life drains out of me and I see clearly the book that I will never write, I see my son, the single sharp shooting pain between one heartbeat and another, I see time, a soft ribbon that keeps coming undone.

There is a suppression of spaces, a shrinking of perspectives, these are the same nightfalls as in my childhood, with terror and horses, the same nightfalls as in my adolescence, with illnesses and verses. Everything about me is rejuvenated for death. Instead of clothing us in extravagant Baroque draperies, time strips us bare. Everything is a gradual return to childhood, to simplicity, for death does not get any bigger as life and pain confer their decorations on us. We are children, innocent and alone when death overtakes us, and it is at moments such as these, as the darkness gathers, that I may die.

We accumulate things as we erect a bulwark against death. The delight at possessing nothing is immediately succeeded by the terror of being free of all attachments, all ready to depart. It is imperative to let out anchors, to put out mooring lines, to tie ourselves desperately to life. But I continue to lie here, defenseless, with no desires and no future, between the past and death, between the child and nothingness. Someone has seen literature as childhood recaptured. That's why I write, of course, because to write is to play and to play is to be the quintessential child. The one and only adventure I seek is childhood, mine and that of the world, that of my son and of sons everywhere. I want only the play, the wheeling of the planet. I witness the games of these children of the street without actually seeing them. I am not the smiling, condescending observer, but the human space in which they play, all of mankind attentively following their game, heaven and earth, the city and its lights. Saved from desire by the recent blaze, esthetically purified by sex, I listen to my life reduced to its minimum and ultimate possibility, I am the very least I can possibly be, and saved from time for a few moments, saved in space, I am nothing but the warm dusk and the blue shadow in which the children play.

OCTOBER. The world becomes more perfectly round. The trees are violins whose music is the sky. The woods play with my son like a green tiger playing with a linnet. We are the inside of an apple falling slowly and silently in time.

Sometimes I watch the days going by like hollow spaces, the adolescent light drying in the treetops, the relief of time bursting with seed sculpted in young girls, and the miracle of everything that is invisibly taking on solid form. I look at the warm gold that is left behind when children lose their innocence in the afternoon, and with beggar's hands I slowly collect the color of music and the air of life.

Your body is a beautiful fragment
of some shattered unknown grandeur.
The fruit basket of your life
replenishes itself all by itself each day.
In your mangled mouth the sadness
*   of Tuesdays speaks*
and in your meticulous fingers pages of light
*   are set ablaze.*
You make the world denser, like a plant
*   growing too luxuriantly*
and give off wave upon wave of intense perfume
*   where no one passes.*
You have rusted the air with your weariness,
you have buried all the clarinets,
you have ruined breasts, like antiquities,
and harvest thighs that weigh heavily on the day.
I seek in your soul a tobacco of childhood days,
I seek in your sex a breathless sea,
and I see how the dead, subletting your house,
lend a slightly happier note
to love's destruction and the kitchen's emptiness.

I return from my travels, my son, I return from the world, all iron and wine, and I find you here, in the tender heart, in the cool interior of the fruit that your life is. When you are far away, I always feel you at the root of everything, I experience you behind everything I experience, and I need only go off to a distant foreign country for you to turn into the warm, vulnerable center of the turning world. Cities, trains, sidewalks, days, women, clothes, fruit, living-machines, everything revolves about you, the soft interior, the close-hauled sails of life. To travel is to beat around the bush, to exile oneself from the center, to circle around an interior that sends out its call to us. When I return to you, to your eyes that fight against the darkness, to your voice that opens naturally, like a lotus on the surface of life's waters, I sense that I have come back to the warm center of the planet. How cold it is outside, son, what a desolation of stone cities, fallen heavens, shattered times, vegetable people, and clamorous mineral days.

How comfortable it is here. The world, I now know, has an inside made of wool and conversation, laughter and play, in which you live, carefully hidden away. I need only go away for a short time for you to turn into the center of heaven and earth. I hear your voice, the volatile incoherence of what you say, possessed of much more sense and music than all the systems read about in books and endlessly debated. It does not matter that you imitate the world in the games you play. It is playing and miracle that make you a secret fountain. Everything is falling down on an immense scale, whereas you are making your way upward slowly, one tiny step at a time. The world is undergoing a tremendous, tragic collapse, the inverse of each one of your heartbeats as you grow toward the light.

❡ 66

• • •

When I read, in the quiet solitude of the house, in the
silence of the night, or in the still white light of an afternoon
absorbed in thought, my little boy lies sleeping, and everything
takes its rest in his slumber, the discourse of the book flows
over this pure white bed of a child's sleep. How the world,
so exhausted, so heavy, depends on the light sleep of children
to support it. My son's slumber is the murmur of the world,
the ultimate lightness of life, and the battles of the prose I
am reading rage back and forth above the twofold innocence
of a sleeping child.

My son is in the market, amid the clamor of the fruit,
burned by all the fires of fresh things, illuminated by all the
smells of the countryside. Fruit communicates its health to
him by contagion, though only for a moment, alas, and the
little boy laughs, looks, touches, runs about, unconsciously
aware of a natural world, the pruned grove in which he finds
himself, and the products of live, growing trees that a basket
of fruit, a fruit stall represents. My son in the market, amid
the early-morning crime of butchered meat, amid the silent
fires of the fruit, setting him ablaze with their greens, reds,
mauves, yellows. My little boy, a fruit that speaks, a living
pumpkin, is now caught in a crossfire, pinned down by the
thousand cold fires of fruit, and he shouts, screams, laughs,
lives, suddenly possessed of a host of natural relatives, a cousin
of peaches, a brother of tomatoes, with moments when he is a
vegetable and moments when he is an exquisite tropical fruit.
It is as if we had taken him to visit a house where a big
family of relatives lives, a home with many children. It is
like running into a noisy horde of young cousins again. What
a din of colors in the fruit market! The child runs amid the
fruits, amid the children, amid the cousins, amid the apricots.

Letters, the alphabet, the scale of vowels, the child, in
his mother's shadow, a little bird flitting about in the tree of

grammar. He hops here, there, and everywhere, lands on the wrong branch, hops again, says *a, e,* laughs with the *i,* is frightened by the *u,* lives.

That is where the story begins, my son, where culture begins, the human world, that long game that we have invented in order to postpone death. Letters, those likable, stubborn insects, play with you like ants that are difficult partners. You are beginning to play letters as if they were a musical instrument, the keys of a piano that have resounded through five or ten millennia.

Each letter bears within it an echo of past languages, of tongues thousands of years old, that you awaken in all innocence, as if you were singing inside a catacomb. You are the paleontologist of our world of hieroglyphs. We are your distant ancestors, Egyptian sphinxes, Greek gods, Etruscan statues, Nubian dialects. I feel, alas, more like one of your ancestors of antiquity than one of your recent forebears. Embodied in me is a culture centuries old, a fossil that looks down, undaunted, on your joyous bird-hops across the gravestones of the past. Each letter is a gravestone you step on, each word a tomb. You are playing games in the cemetery, like the children in that famous film, for words are corpses, funerals, a way of embalming things. You, who a short time ago still belonged to the bright new realm of things, are now unwittingly entering the dark realm of words, of signs.

But signs and words, for you, are also things, for your contact with reality is all of a piece, wholesome and salutary, and you play with letters as you play with insects or pebbles. I don't know if you should be torn away from the world of things. I don't know if you will live a long life in the world of ideas or in any world, my son, but I witness, in sorrow and dismay, your reaching the point where borders meet, where one forecourt joins another, and watch you cross them joyously, holding your mother's hand.

You come from the realm of birds and are headed for the tomb. You come from the vegetable realm and are headed toward the realm of the conceptual. You don't know, my son, how difficult it is to make language a sensual pleasure, a discovery, a fruit once again. The path leading back that you are just now starting on is a long one. Will you have time to reach the end?

I would like to journey along this path with you, my son. Neither you nor I will be able to reach the end of it, surely. Neither of us will live long enough, perhaps, you because you started along it too soon and I because I started along it too late. It makes me happy, it saddens me, it pains me, it upsets me to see you playing with fire, with the dismal quenched fire of words, even though in your hands and in your voice it blazes brightly once again: live flames, happiness, conflagration, madness, song.

My *a* is not your *a*. My *a* is gloomy and full of solemn wisdom learned from books. Your *a* is a night of pure light in your palate, in the clear palate of the world. What a play of lights and shadows. At times language hovers threateningly over you, and I am terrified. At times you trap it under a net of confusion as you play joyous games with it. What fear, what happiness, what sadness I feel as I see you learning your letters.

That afternoon in spring or autumn—autumnal spring, April-like autumn—when we were on the boundary line between the city and the country, with a cemetery in the background, vast, immense, vertical, a valley of the dead and cypresses, and my son in the Sunday light, a shipwreck victim amid poppies, wheat fields on the outskirts of the city, ears of corn and corncobs, rubble, people picnicking and people alone, a great ugly district of the city that ended there, and in the other direction, toward the east, the highway linking the city with its cemetery outpost, so that its dead can be buried in the countryside.

How my little boy ran, how he sang, how he played. How

clearly I could see him, against the unreal yet sharply outlined background of the cemetery, taking part in the pathetic fiesta, picking his way through the rubble, looking for flowers among the stones, for stones among the flowers. A violet sky that soon became a night sky, and the vague feeling of relief I had on taking the child's hand and returning with him to the city, rescuing him from I know not what distant realms of the dead and open fields.

So it was many times, returning from the sad fiesta at the end of the week, with the child hoisted in my arms, heavy with sleep, amid people doing nothing for a day, boarding trains, buses, streetcars, getting off them, returning home, carrying the bundle of his fatigue against my chest, as on the way out of the city, in the happiness of the first hours, he had carried the bundle of his laughter and his radiance, which little by little leaked away. How much a child ages on a weekend. How a Sunday wilts him.

A son, the leap the day takes
toward another day.
A hop-skip-and-jump
A heel-and-toe-and-away-we-go
A cartwheel in the air
toward another air.
The weeks for you take zigzag steps
Missing all the cracks:
Step on a crack, break your mother's back.
When the world has no idea
where to turn next
and everything stops dead
as though bound in iron fetters
you leap, both feet together,
and clear the wall,
and then the day begins to flow again
crystal water in your water.

I know you, the girl said, I know you, she said vaguely in the mist, with thick lips of emptiness. And there she was in ner thicket of fog, with the burning dog at her side, looking at me. I know you, I know you, in the cold, very cold morning, entangled in wisps of fog, and I, with my pain, my fear, my loneliness, my uncertainty, halted in front of her, I remember, full of sudden desire. I know you, I know you, and she had heavy hair with a part down the middle, hard black eyes, a face rejuvenated by the cold, the contours of a statue of an adolescent, the indistinctness of language and of mist. The dog at her side was a fire in the shape of a dog, burning in the freezing morning, calling through its eyes and mouth. I know you, I know you.

I could have taken a step forward, touched the blackness of that face with my hand, destroyed the image, reduced it to a sandstone block of reality, of truth. But my hand remained suspended, weightless, in the air, closely watched by the dog, and we parted. I know you, I know you. She was a woman of the wilds in the frozen heart of the city, she was a clay more wholesome than beautiful. But how distant she was. On one of the coldest and most painful mornings of my life, my love, my desire for that creature related by marriage to her loathsome dog was doubtless destined to remain unfulfilled.

The blood of the wound, pain wandering through my body like a blind gray bat, fever, fear, that is what I am, that is what you are. If not, what else? We contrive to produce a substance of varying consistency, something rather mediocre, that goes by the names of imagination, literature, esthetics, lyricism, good, faith in mankind, history, freedom, justice. Yet all it takes is this drop of blood, this mute complaint of my body, this red dripping of life, and suddenly everything is blotted out and my entire being is reduced to my pain. I am not my pain, the poet said. I think we are indeed our pain. Pain, blood, fever, fear, the black heralds of death—a death so far off, so distracted—frighten off all the birds in one's head in the space of an instant.

I look at my drop of blood, the miserable little bit of myself that I am shedding, and I observe with a passionate repugnance, with an animal's base love of his animality, how life gushes forth into death, how death gushes forth into life, how close I am at every moment to coming untied and being nothing but nothingness, how loose the sack of my life is. I am water in a basket, a bundle of rain leaking death everywhere.

Suicide? It takes great faith in life to do away with oneself. Suicide is the greatest affirmation of life. If I ever reach the point of killing myself, it will not be for lack of faith, but for the opposite reason. There are only impassioned suicides. For the time being I have made skepticism my abode. My abode till a drop of blood, a shark of fear, rips through my body. The body is a machine for living, and it is pointless to keep warning it that death doesn't matter. The body has one and only one trajectory. One cannot persuade an arrow in flight to change direction.

I am here with my fear. I am a bleeding intestine or a heart burning up with fever. Philosophy, art, ideas, beauty are simply truces between one sickness and another. Sickness is a truce granted by death.

I hoard my blood with love and scorn. Yet in the vortex of horror, when you are nothing but a stone of pain and fear, a mineral of terror, imagination is born, like a flower rooted in rock, the metaphor that turns sickness into metaphor, the distanced vision of yourself. Distance is esthetics. Can terror produce lilies? I am certain it can. What am I, then, who am I? All this physiology has engendered the ineffable. All these fruits of death have brought forth a dream-flower: imagination, the evil beauty of the world seen through my eyes. Thought is nothing more than a continuation of the necessities of the jungle. Lyric emotion frees itself of all necessity. The essence of man: lyric emotion.

This blood, then? I touch my dried blood, I touch my injured body, and I am reassured by the evidence, even though it is a proof of death.

WHAT a bonfire of sun noon is, what a Sunday of smoke and airplanes. My son, amid the white blazes of autumn, with a fife, a whistle, a balloon, passing through glazes of smoke, blocks of sky, multitudes sitting eating, a heavenly glory of charred animal flesh and a ceiling of planes wrought of silver and speed. What a November Sunday, clear and cold. Walking through towns celebrating a day off, amid picnickers in flames, seeing my son walking, immortal for a moment, in a golden halo of noon, blind with light, through the fields, the water, the smoke, the air, the world.

The three of us were happy for a moment in the great fat cloud of charred meat, in the sudden intense blaze of Sunday.

We were lyrical and white, two graceful souls in a paper spring. Remember? Now life has brought us together, seared by the passing days, seasoned with death. We were among the chosen who made the light glow, and one day, one of those days that pass in shadow, life brought us together. What a great meeting of souls, what a way of consummating belatedly what had barely begun earlier. Time had ripened you for me. The thousand women that you were or had been stood between us, but we killed them off one by one with shots of booze and the knives of our voices, until we came back to time recaptured. I don't know. The sun that brought out your freckles like a gratuitous flowering had dulled your eyes and counted your hair over again, but I contrived, we contrived, to make you the same as before. A stone that ached just a little more now, you poured forth the same water of your cool voice, the same clear, liquid sound.

I want to taste bodies that death has already tasted with a gluttony that forewarns me of nothing. After the first lick of death's tongue on my flesh, I want other mouths to sanctify it with life. I wanted to count the freckles on your body once more, that same day long ago when we met, as you came from the past or the future, I don't know which. Men, lights, fears, loves had passed through your body, which recognized me, despite all, as the sea would recognize the first vessel—wood and dreams—that parted it in the early light of dawn.

The past became entangled with the present for us, life with death, but I witnessed in your weary eyes the spectacle of some trivial things, such as the darkness of a certain shade of green, or the slowness of certain glances. In an ever-changing universe, the intimate spectacle of stability is fascinating: a voice that continues to fall from the same cataracts of foam, a pair of eyes that continues to take in the same golden and amber lights.

What is responsible for the identity of a being, of a woman, whose cells, whose life, whose heart change each day? Some would say it is the soul. An explanation that explains nothing. Another name for mystery. How stubbornly we remain ourselves. All we need do is see a person, meet him again in time, to realize to our stupefaction that he lives his life as a prisoner of his voice, his movements, his laugh. Or that he keeps going back over the same ground, repeating all these things, assiduously, lovingly, without realizing it. We are at once the stone and the sea that polishes it. We round off the corners of ourselves every day. As time goes by we become ourselves more and more. Some philosophers call this the process of individuation. Another name for the soul. We are as fixed as a tree, as clearly defined as a stone. The changes within us are slight ripples on the surface of the water, on the surface of our skin. Feelings change, experience puts out black flags, but there is a luminous stone from which the look in our eyes is born, there is a quivering water from which our laughter is born, which are ever the same within the cavern of being.

I found that in you, in her, in her body, in her life as she lived it. I dipped into the green cavern of her being deeper than before, much deeper, but the light and dark bottom, green and alive, was intact, adolescent, the same as always. I had reached what doesn't change. I had gotten nowhere.

An intense slice, your body, a bramble patch of freckles, a red and white and gold fiesta, that I remember now, so far yet so close, like a mad fountain of my life. If only I had sunk my teeth into the broken cry of your life, into the soft thread of your soul, torn you apart into names, sighs, kisses. A fresh greenness of days, a mouth of light, an apple. The heavy glory of your body, a warm patch of plowed earth from which voice-birds took wing.

THE subway is a speeding, flashing darkness, an infiltration, dripping water, life. A person who travels by subway at the age of forty is a failure. If one has a coin one changes it, you said to yourself, and the clattering wheels of the subway repeated the phrase. Outcroppings of shadow, human walls, the descent into the subway, what an immersion in the swift catacomb of the ages.

The subway, an immense uterus throbbing with hordes of people, smells, salesgirls, advertising posters, and the subway employee with a blank look under his Metropolitan Transit Company cap, releasing the gas, blowing the whistle, opening and closing the swinging doors, like a horizontal guillotine putting to death the human monster with a thousand heads.

Love in the subway, the hands like sausages gripping the overhead bar, entering or leaving a moving car strictly forbidden, allow passengers leaving the car to get off before entering, no peddling permitted in subway trains, and the bas-relief of faces, the clay of life divided up into grimaces, fatigues, laughs, stupefactions, mouths. Steeped in depth, hermetically sealed in speed, obstinately anonymous, the silent majority of the world above, the nocturnal fauna of the world below, each head with its aureole of smell, suffering, hair, souls like cheap cologne, bodies like sacks worn thin, and the hidden flowers of armpits and the secret urine of years.

We ride on the subway with a piece of paper in our pockets, with the message of life, with the letter of recommendation or the bill for the furniture, and the alluvial deposit of mothers, petty functionaries, youngsters, beggars. A vast fresco of the city, an immense mural of faces in the subway car, humanity in tempera, in spray paint, and the swift catastrophe of the subway, its ugliness of iron rattling against iron, until the poor girl's unexpected smile, the sun of the lower depths on a woman's hair, or the quiet, conspiratorial waters of glances exchanged between you and me.

There are all sorts down in the subway, as you know, so watch out for men who look suggestively at other men, and take refuge in that working girl's face, in that bramble patch of freckles, in the young girl who's a presser, a messenger, an office clerk, an apprentice, in the girl without a steady job whose profile trembles in the glaring subterranean light and whose eyes are full of advertisements. You moved closer to her when the hordes poured out of the subway, and your silence full of meaning was louder than all the talk going on in the car, let them give it to the idiot where he likes it, five duros is all I've got left, he's always broke, that man, Doña Águeda, what are we going to do with him if the Social Security people don't pension him off?

A block of silence between you and me, a sandbar with toothless snatches of conversation, till the last station, or the station where you got off, with a slight turn of your profile toward me, and though I didn't know whether this was meant as an invitation or a farewell, I nonetheless followed you and we emerged on a public square full of pensioners, a vast crowded quarter of the city, with lots of trucks and wine casks ready for the scrap heap in the middle of the street. It was your neighborhood. How difficult it was to break the steel of silence that had been forged between us, after having seen you mount the stairs of the subway station with the grace of a working-class gazelle, and your legs dancing as they walked along, and a suburban paradise, with vegetable gardens and little workshops. It isn't true that you held out your rough child's hand to me and saved me forever among your neighborhood suns and sunflowers. The truth is, rather, that I am here in the subway again, eternally in the subway, just as it isn't true that another life is passing through me, another time, brighter weather. If one has a coin one changes it. Life is a lofty, sunny dream only for those of us who travel by subway, for those of us who imagine a world up above with children and good weather.

The subway man dreams of a city of sun and leisure that he never leaves. The city of statues and bars is a nightmare to the man of the world below, to the passenger buried deep underground, to the man who travels by subway, you, me, this seat reserved for crippled war veterans, we are all crippled war veterans, the terrible-tempered mothers with bulging shopping bags, the little girl reading a big fat book, the messenger boy whistling in the subway, and the field sown with heads that I see below me, a bald head with continents outlined on it, a thick mane with bright glints in it, the four hairs on a milky-white skull, the trace of the curling iron in a woman's gray hair, ashes crimped in tenuous waves of resignation, and the violent corn-yellow of a young girl's hair, a plump adolescent who gives off sweet fragrance and light.

No, the city doesn't exist, the city is a fit of madness, an invention, a hope, a lie. A dream dreamed down below by those who travel by subway, souls in purgatory in a tunnel, the just crowded together elbow to elbow, a dank limbo, a swift catacomb. We don't exist, we don't drink coffee, we don't make love. We are merely dreamed, *de profundis,* by a silent man traveling by subway.

On foggy afternoons, when I walked through the city amid a multitude of luminous, vague, floating eyes to your house, I found myself among bakeries and record shops, and then took an old, slow street elevator that passed by vast courtyards, houses without walls, beams spanning the open air, immense spaces for hanging the washing out to dry, thus finally reaching the silence of a green bedroom with fish hung from the ceiling, a basket full of rotten fruit, wind on the terrace, and an open, bleeding book. Your usual hairdo, parted in the middle, combed by loneliness, and your alcohol eyes, a dark, tired tobacco color, the passionate clay of your face, your large debauched mouth, stories of love affairs, memories of memories, hard warm hands, a body full of sex and resentment. And as the novel of words, of reproaches, of dreams was consummated, I fell in love with your tiny, simple, practical foot, whose one beauty was its reduction to essentials.

All the old worn-out psychologizing, the sad story of love, the heart's games, all the things that the novelists of the past studied in minute detail by the light of their bourgeois kerosene lamps, I study in darkness, or in a monologue with you, while I am really in love with your foot, thinking of your foot, not daring to say that life is unimportant, that feelings are reversible, and that the only living, appealing reality was your bare foot, pure as a stone, self-assured as a little animal, golden as a summer.

These are mere incidental details. You were the blind vessel sending back a weary echo, the pale violinist, much whiter than yourself, you were love in asymmetrical bedrooms, the unadorned nakedness of bare light bulbs, the cold water in unused kitchens, a smell of oil paint and next-door neighbors, or that blond mane you had, that I had, no longer your dark hair with a part in the middle, but a spilling out of gold and music, a long, soft, sick body making its way along my body, the touch of a knowing mouth, destruction in the guise of intercourse, the ruin of a young architecture, what a mysterious fiesta of blood and light.

Or you were the bramble patch of freckles—who were you, who are you, to whom am I addressing myself, what am I writing?—the fallen apple, a love with many mirrors, overpowering, stifling furniture, boy dolls, the cold, childish gaze of one decorative object or another, and a body that had recovered, a glory about to burst into flame, a laugh that even today makes your optimistic, tired flesh glow. I don't know whom I am talking about, what unfolding, what protean multiplication of forms: a continual bright chorus of women in your life, always a woman, a sword of fire, a bold archangel, a naked body, laying siege to your life, illuminating you. I remember what it was like when you came back, after night had fallen, mist in the mist, your body alive with the whip marks, your eyes burned from being so close to flesh, and your nostrils intoxicated by the mingling of perfume and blood.

From what woman, from what battle were you returning, while I was alone in the darkness pierced by car headlights, the light of the body fading from my mind, making me opaque, heavy, dark, real. With a renewed natural fire you were setting days ablaze, like old crackling logs, specially marked as you felled the deep forest that you were, recognizing yourself.

Serena, slender and agile, watches the night go by with quiet eyes, smiling, and her outline of a vessel glows with the lights of lovemaking and alcohol. Everything is on fire around her, yet the flames scarcely touch the granite of her sadness. Serena silently watches time pass, kisses, hands, lights, loves, until the bonfire of the night burns down to embers and neither sleep nor love comes to her quiet eyes.

Serena, slender and agile, visits the shops in the late afternoon, undresses in the fitting rooms, puts on and takes off red or white linen garments, as the mirrors of big department stores sing to her in a confusion of buckles and mannequins. Serena smokes an acrid tobacco, or allows her naked body to burn in the mirror of the fitting room, as the city lights up with umbrellas. Serena, tall, lithe, white, blond, sits naked at the piano, unleashing notes like blackbirds, or makes herself tea on the portable heater, or masturbates with the shower water. Serena cries out as she mounts an attack or makes love, and Beethoven gazes at her in silence as she applies lotions, creams, and lights to her white body. She cohabits with sparrows that sleep in the piano and hides lamps under the bed. Serena, ocher-colored and freckled, laughs or sings amid the cataract of cars. Serena, cider and laughter, speaks in the vitals of trains, competes on dizzying grand-prix circuits, visits the snow on mountaintops, or weeps silent green tears. Serena, satiated and lonely, downs the alcohol of guilt and sleeps amid boy dolls and celluloid. Serena blond, Serena brunette, Serena heavy, Serena light, Serena haughty, Serena intimate, a woman's footsteps walking through the city, and this song to the solitary creature, to femininity that is erectile, to the erosion of light decanting or consuming bodies.

Or that woman who came to the city from her province, dressed to the hilt in old elegances, the same being continually reincarnated in successive bodies, that disconcerting resemblance of life to itself, feminine calligraphies of dawn, sad lives, the pale message of a solitary, ordinary creature who one day becomes a presence, hairdo, furs, the childlike solemnity with which she invests everything, the importance of what she is experiencing, that importance that I must play a role in, or rather, that I must preside over, my infinite reluctance and remoteness, when will we be free, wild waves breaking over an unknown rock, not this whole lamentable ritual display of sentiment, these admirations that are of no use to me at this point, and what's more make me feel like a comically monstrous, evil person, moved by a cheap, petty satanism that fills me with a sense of utter humiliation, mediocrity, and weariness.

The thought of a nymph, something to redeem me from such loves, a refreshing shower of youth and freedom, I don't know; maybe, I thought, you're losing your interest in women, your zest for love adventures. An ordinary woman is like a bad book: it makes you distrust all literature, everything feminine. Shadows that go back home, sad fires that you should never have kindled, and the meeting, like a unique and total liberation, with the clear, bright winter day, uncut crystal, a block of time, a frozen Sunday, and here I am strolling about through the loneliness with my body absent, without a past and without a future, clean of every last trace of a woman, empty of lust, neither sad nor happy.

The painter is here, the painter lights cigars, snuffs them out, drains the big glass of cognac, sets it down again. The painter works with his fingernails, with his fingers, with scraps of old paper, with bricklayer's tools, with color directly, surrounded by a choir of neighborhood arcades, wrecked houses, dreary courtyards. At the top of an ancient, rickety staircase, the painter sets red on fire, combines subtle shades of green, creates yellow, invents black, deepens the orange tones, enriches the grays, dreams blue. The painter has a gray, red, unruly, powerful, unkempt head of hair, a stubborn, submerged pate, and he fills his canvas with a strong sea breeze, making it billow like a sail. Dripping faucets, sick walls, empty kitchens, the winter song of toilets, and nothing but this intense heat of paint, this blaze of colors, a comical, lyrical, fat, cruel, ugly, visionary being born in the fervent piling up of layer on layer of oil paint.

The painter lights cigars, gulps cognac, complains, laughs, goes down the stairs, lazily climbs them again, talks into chipped telephones, repeats women's names, sings, reads newspapers, sleeps on his side, quarrels, gets into fights, goes downstairs to the street, comes back upstairs, buys, sells, has visions, loves humanity or holds it in contempt, and then goes on painting. The painter is there before my eyes, brimming over with energy, entirely given to his painting, or preoccupied with ulcers, full to bursting with wine and medicine, a ripeness boiling over, painting, painting. Fingernails black with paint, a soul full of oil and turpentine, eyes full of time, a messy, mixed-up jumble of life, offspring, love, painting, friends, windows, women, and illnesses. The painter makes his lonely way down lighted streets, converses with strangers, thinks long thoughts about ghosts and suicide, reads nineteenth-century literature, and has a kind heart and a battle of colors in his head that he leaves behind in his room, day after day, until a person is born of his loneliness.

The painter, the friend, there before my eyes, the spectacle of a man being burned alive in a thousand fires, the way a life is consummated and consumed, the way the fire that kills is the fire that creates. That may be what art is: this fatal fire, domesticated by a hand that gives it permanent form and fulfills it. The material that devours him is the material with which he paints. Then he turns out the lights, turns one on again for one last look at the painting, closes the door, goes down the stairs and out into the street, leaving behind a wake of courtyards, light, color, pain, and words. He reigns in a world of crumpled newspapers, he stands at bars downing drinks, he eyes women, he pisses mournfully and buys himself a paintbrush that he will never use. A life in the process of combustion, a fire fed by tobacco, medicine, words, love-making, and siestas. The painter is more hemmed in by things than other men are, more trapped amid volumes and forms; everything signals to him, he sees fires in everything. The painter sees more of the world than we do, he has a more intimate knowledge of the physiognomy of life, he awakens colors and gestures. That's how we would like to write, with the painter's directness and plasticity, without falling into the gray, complacent realm of ideas. The painter storms about before me, creating blindly and attacking the canvas with his whip, punishing it to stay alive, not to die, to bleed black blood and suffer green wounds.

The writer is working on his long book. He is driving his car through the fog, against the oncoming lights and the rain, he is driving with fractured, injured, bandaged hands and talking to me about his book, about love, about life. What is he searching for? Where is he going?

The writer cleaves the night with his machine, drives with aching hands, touches his nose, his eyes, talks—his book, his endless book, women, travels, a beach in England, walking through the woods, words in Latin—the writer is searching for something. I have no idea what, and neither does he. How meaningless, how insane the searching of others is. And what of our own? Does he see me as I see him, lost, anxious, alone? Capturing life in a book, taking time's measurements. That's writing. Giving conventional dimensions to existence. One manipulates time for artistic effect, thus ruling, falsely, secretly, over one's own life. Time races on when one gives it free rein. One must catch it in the rat trap (time is a rat) of a book, a project, a trip somewhere. The writer dreams of a book, a woman, a distant city. The details are all wrong. We drive through the snow, the rain, the fog. Where are we going? The writer never finishes his book. It is out of fear, out of cowardice, that certain writers leave books unfinished. There is another sort of writer—I for one—who stretches one book over an entire lifetime. When I finish one book, I begin another immediately. One cannot allow the blood of time to drain away drop by drop. The book, the project. So as not to be without a book, without a project, out in the storm, in the rushing torrent of days.

A woman, a book, a city. The writer's age-old myths. The woman, the city, where time stops. The book made with the time of one's life. Putting time to use. But time leaks out of books, women, cities. It continues to flow. The writer drives fast, slowly. Gray sparks set his hair on fire. His nose becomes more sensitive, his hands on the wheel continue to ache, his mouth twitches. He suffers.

The writer, the friend. The writer's blood is time. The painter's blood is light. The writer, the painter, friends. Lives that burn before my life, time that is consumed—are they witnesses of the spectacle of my time, of the conflagration of my life? As we burn ourselves out, we give off a light that only others can see. We go through life in flames, and nobody warns us that we are on fire so as not to frighten us. We slowly make our way through the city amid patches of light and darkness, heading nowhere, talking, dreaming, braving the cold, fear, shadows, driving past vast holes of time, streets fast asleep, multitudes.

It is snowing again.

My little boy in the white prison of the clinic, in the manip-
ulating, jabbing hands of pain, the child suffering among
other children who are suffering. They have entered life
through the yellow tunnel of sickness. The child, my child,
is there, in pain, brought face to face with a fear, with something much bigger than himself, and they carry him from
place to place in dirty white wings, they trundle him about
in hard, creaking stretcher-beds. I refuse to love a creation
in which children are tortured, a French writer said. I keep
remembering this, and I repeat it each time my little boy
is in pain. *Creation*. A sinister word written with a capital
letter, incarnating suffering in a child's flesh. The useless fury
that life vents upon life. Trapped in the maw of pain, with
death staring him in the face, the child's eyes shatter into bits
of crystal, his hands, no longer flowerlike, grow bony, and the
inhuman pallor of sheer terror comes over him. The universe
is a gratuitous geometry, an insane, intransigent mathematics,
blindly fulfilling its laws, vainly demonstrating itself to itself,
and a child in pain, a victim, is always needed to keep this
pointless play of useless forces going. The pain of children,
the pain of plants, the pain of animals. How intolerable these
three kinds of pain are. The child suffers the way beasts and
plants suffer. Emitting feeble cries and a fragrance.

The clinic is a green corridor where for a brief moment
pain becomes reasonable. Science has rationalized pain to a
modest degree, and has become puffed up with pride at doing
so. The universe, creation, a prodigious machine for churning
out errors, a perfect closed system of mistakes, is a vast absurdity tantamount to a rational principle underlying everything. It works. It runs on the pain and death of children and
is lubricated by the fresh blood of children. I take my little

boy, weak and in pain, far from the great organized absurdity, to our little corner of unreasonableness, to our secret lair of tenderness. He is numb with fear, bewildered by the cold, but he begins to put things in order—his own warm, chaotic order.

Suddenly, you see what you have always dreamed of and experienced so often: a huge lecture hall, an enormous crowd awaiting you, as in a dream, a grove of youthful heads, a ravine of torsos, an atmosphere of expectancy, and also something threatening in the air. The audience, the people, the thousand heads, the thousands of eyes that you wanted to have focused on you when you were an adolescent are now there before you, repeatedly, one day, and another and another, waiting, waiting, waiting—for what?

What can I tell them, how can I live up to their expectations? The attention you dreamed of. You have their attention now, but it turns out that a crowd is always sinister, even though it has come to drink in your words. How do you plunge deep within them, how do you play this huge, multiple body like an instrument, with a word, a gesture, so that the entire powerful, quivering surface of the monster will begin to undulate?

The child, the youngster I was, dreamed of this attention, dreamed of this silence awaiting his words, this expectation focused entirely on him. All this has come about, like a dream come true, and it is neither grandiose nor beautiful nor intoxicating. On the contrary: it is gloomy, somber, sinister. You have contrived to make thousands of heads turn toward you, and you have nothing to say to them. It is as if any moment now, in their fury at having been fooled, they will seize you and tear you to pieces. The dream of the ideal that the youngster you were bore within him is nothing but an ignoble need to dominate. To be successful, to enjoy what the world calls success, is to subjugate. Every success is a form of aggression. Glory is an act of murder, fame an act of violence, popularity an act of hostility. Imposing a self on another self, penetrating that other self, raping it, twisting it, making it turn into me. Taming crowds is a strange métier, as strange as taming snakes or elephants. That force there in front of me is latent and multiple. I contrive to hypnotize it for a moment. Is that what success is, a form of hypnosis? Absolutely. The magic spell cast over this audience will eventually be broken and they will be free again, they will be themselves. In the crowd are young boys who might be my friends, young girls who might be my mistresses. Such a relationship would be cordial, natural, spontaneous, human, genuine. The relationship that fame establishes is false, monstrous, base. An act of subjugation takes place. I see blond heads, gray heads, the unruly tresses of youth and the tidy ashes of maturity. I never become accustomed to the sight of this crowd before me.

I will be someone else, I will be aggressive, I will strum upon the stagnant water that I have turned them into, that I have bewitched them into becoming, until the deep lake sings or laughs with me. But I am depressed, sad, frightened, conscience-ridden, remorseful. To turn a crowd into a vast pool of eyes is to humiliate the individual human being, to attack the entire human race. As I have no way of fulfilling the expectation that I have patiently aroused over the years, I will shine lights in their eyes to bring them out of the spell I have cast over them, before they wake to the fact that they are beside themselves with fury, a multitude, a monster. The monster has come to feed on me; like human octopuses, their eyes and mouths seek me out. They are here to destroy me and I am here to bewitch them. They are here to suck a soul dry, to drain the expression in a pair of eyes, my eyes, to the very last drop, to drink from them like eagles, to swallow up my words the way a big fish swallows up little fish. They don't know that the force that unites them is a destructive one, for admiration is also destruction.

Love and death, love and hate, love and destruction. And the love of a thousand men and women for one man? Admiration, expectation. I assert myself at their expense, and they take their sustenance from me, they are out to feed on my soul and my vitals. Collective admiration is sublimated hatred, unconsummated destruction.

History teaches us, to our surprise, that the masses who adore a leader stone him to death later on. There is nothing inconsistent here. The two phenomena are essentially the same. Adoration is a form of possession, and possession is consummated only in destruction.

We can adore only what we have destroyed. The key to the Christian temperament, the best explanation of it, is found in the guilt that underlies it. A man is killed, a God, whereupon he can be venerated through the ages. The murder of the father marks the beginning of religion. Any enduring form of worship requires the leaven of guilt.

They have come en masse to hear me, and they might well stone me to death because there is a human appetite for the human that can be satisfied only through delirium or blood. To provoke the delirium of the crowd is to defend oneself against its ferocity. When the delirium ends, they will kill me. The animal tamer enters the cage of wild beasts with a torch. His life will last as long as the torch keeps burning. Fire fascinates lions. But they will then devour this fascination. The relationship between the public figure and his followers is similar.

I am not talking of the childish fear of timid lecturers, but of the deep fear a child feels when he has aroused a sleeping dog. The need to awaken it, and then the terror of seeing that it's awake. How one longs to be unknown, anonymous once again. What a relief to go through life in silence, greeting only one's friends. This great solid block of expectation falls to pieces once I have finished speaking, and individuals come up to speak to me, a student, an elderly lady, a gentleman, a pretty woman. The magic spell is broken, the audience is no longer bewitched, they are persons once again, freed of their mass identity and the great solid block. Expectation is then manifested in ordinary little ways, a book, a signature, a greeting, a smile, a few words exchanged, a hand-shake. This is the innocent, petty-bourgeois form of popularity. It amounts to nothing, serves no purpose. The Greek tragedy of the multitude degenerated into a comedy of manners: the writer and his public. How fond I am of my public once they are persons again, once they have faces and voices. I have something in common with them now. The circus act that we have all had a hand in, they and I, has vanished in thin air.

Crowds are dizzying, tempting, dangerous. The sheer presence of the crowd generates an anxiety comparable only to the anxiety that overcomes us when we are confronted with the naked body of a woman. Too auspicious. These hundreds of persons are a forest, and the secret pyromaniac in our blood would like to see the forest set on fire, to make a mass meeting, a stirring anthem, a flag, an apotheosis, a war out of it. Faced with a crowd, the writer confines himself to giving a lecture. Later, in my solitude, peopled by books, silences, and the presence of my son, it is not trophies of glory that I hold in my hands, but an emptiness, the awareness of a vast mistake, of a misunderstanding that falls far short of being tragic. A simple, ordinary misunderstanding. I am not who they think I am. They are not who I think they are. They dream that they admire me. I dream that they admire me. One dream meets another.

Violence stalks the streets, the dark surging sea of politics, and the wing of fear brushes past again in the night, blood and pain sing, human beings clot, light trampling on light, shadow on shadow. Something is happening. This is how history makes its way, my son. In fits and starts, stumbling along, driven forward with bloody blows of the lash and cries of hatred. There are days when I see clearly the dialectical progress of the world, the broadening of horizons, the dawning lights of the future. But on other days everything is black, son, threatened with imminent doom, blinded by the inevitability of fate.

¶ 92

The world sits comfortably poised on exploitation and moves only when shifted out of balance by war. The world comes to a halt and rests on the backs of the exploited, or marches on trampling corpses underfoot. Underfoot are the quicksands of vast expanses of suffering men. Desolate wastelands of blood illuminate our landscape.

Do we move forward in circles, in straight lines, in zigzags? Do we in fact move forward at all? Look closely at a worker. Behind him is a genealogy of plagues, centuries inlaid, in his hands, in his forehead, like tiles in a mosaic.

Leisure, beauty, culture blur the past. Those who would like to be taken for illustrious figures, aristocrats of ancient lineage, in fact lack a tradition, a history. It's the poor in whom history is truly inscribed.

Battles, labor, suffering. The history of sickness and the history of monuments. Everything is there in the body of a worker. They have moved the world. Stitched into their bare breasts are prehistoric ice ages, medieval famines, Roman slavery, Gothic toil, the cursive script of revolutions written in letters of fire, and the black geometry of prisons.

I don't know what I am saying to you, son. I don't know what I am saying to myself. I was saying that violence stalks the streets. Error at times endeavors to fulfill its nature. Or else error aspires to the truth. It wants to realize itself fully as error or redeem itself in certainty. A sense of uneasiness haunts culture, someone said, but I believe that this uneasiness is simply the awareness of our provisional nature. We have reduced the people to a dream. We deny them their reality. Nothing can be founded on the waters of dreams.

One winter follows another. I again have a presentiment that the people want to take on reality, the reality that is denied them, that they want to break the spell that has been cast over them, like a dream or a shadow, like mortar or dirt. Carnivals of blood pass by, and groups in costume celebrate fear. How will we ever reach the noon light, son?

Making my way through unnecessary tunnels, dank cavities, unlucky Sundays, I keep searching for the lyrical white body, the thin woman who scourges like a whip of life, and sometimes, when I fall, disheartened, into buckets of dawn, when in despair I lie smiling in beds made of tin, there suddenly appears, called forth by my loneliness, the creature with invisible breasts, with a musical rump, who submits to lovemaking with the docility of does in spring or sick mares.

I don't know if it is love or the compelling power of my loneliness, I don't know what brings her, I don't know what attracts you, on afternoons fragrant with pain, beneath the shadow of my inflexible down, but it is then that the miracles of heaven, a heaven shorn of its glory and now merely a lowering sky, take place on earth, in high-vaulted grottoes with a marine skylight, or in the vertigo of courtyards where a child has vomited and an old woman has mopped up the blood of the cat she has just killed.

Nothing. The sad proof that these things also happen in life, a man who has realized all his dreams with the strange precision of the sleepwalker, and that female nude who, amid the decrepit jungle of Fridays, sheds a soft light, a light that comes only from the radiance of soul that skin sometimes has, only from the tenuous, pale, young curve of a breast that has not yet fully materialized or a thigh that has disappeared.

As for the rest, days gone mad, pages where time or dust has left its fingerprint, overcoats that fall off coatracks by themselves, like weak-willed suicides, corners where back issues of newspapers and wounded animals live, fiestas in which an innocent tree burns, and boxes of filing cards with a thousand mouths, like dragons ruled off in squares, devouring the perpetuity of paper and the foam rubber of habit. My inside feeds on my outside and vice versa. The young girl has put on a leotard of smoke because she has the chill of cellars in her mauve-colored skeleton.

Making my way through unnecessary tunnels, dank cavities, unlucky Sundays, I return to my lamp of centuries and experience in a rocking chair's movement the disconcerting ease with which life slips by, the indifferent complacency with which dreams are fulfilled, and that twinge of anxiety occasioned by the fact that everything is within my reach, that the painful dreams of the child were only little extra-weekly realities to return to every so often. You can die at any moment with grandiose futility, since you now know that time does its work expeditiously and life gets the necessary formalities over with promptly so it can stand around idly, which is what it likes to do best.

Your body, my girl, was like a warm spring day, thin and indifferent, bright and docile, and though no calendar will perpetuate it, it will glow a bit more brightly beneath the somber paleness of my body, for the mute lamp of your flesh is something that rainy days, ruined streets, and peddlers of poverty know nothing of.

I am seeing a roundness live. A "bottom" and a "behind." Words that suit it very well: that *b* with its straight backbone and its curving loop is a fine symbol of the elasticity, the firmness of what the words are meant to suggest. I am seeing a roundness live. Sometimes when I chance to go out onto the street the roundness suddenly appears in front of me: there she is, walking along in her tight-fitting pants, usually red, and it is unnecessary to see her face to know that it is adorably vulgar, that she has ordinary, mousy brown hair, eyes that are big but lack depth, a little nose, and an impudent mouth. A chick. In the beginning the roundness walks in front of us, we glance at it a couple of times, but we go on with our thoughts. Until we decide to follow it.

In midafternoon, roaming about the city all by myself, I see a roundness live. That rounded *b*, that springiness, that curve and movement that a woman's body has. I have no intention, of course, of catching up with the girl, or of speaking to her. Those days are past. Moreover, it would turn out badly. All I intend to do is to follow along behind her, to watch how that roundness sways back and forth, how it cavorts inside her pants. We don't see a woman who is walking along at our side very well. People approaching in the opposite direction, and especially people walking behind, see her better.

So I decide to walk behind. This is art for art's sake, looking for the sake of looking, following for the sake of following. I wouldn't have anything to say to the girl, except for a few literary figures of speech having to do with her double posterior sphericity, and she wouldn't understand that. She might call a policeman, and he wouldn't understand either.

The disinterestedness, the Platonism, the charm of all this is in following her for a while, in following that roundness, in watching it going up the escalators of department stores, bending over so that the fit of the pants is even tighter, hurrying across the street, appearing and disappearing amid the people on the street. The roundness is perfect, neither too high nor too low, though it is high-slung in relation to her waistline, and rides higher still when it wiggles a little as she walks. It is a roundness that is more spherical than elliptical and is not exaggeratedly curved, and so it is more like an apple than a pear, as is only fitting and proper. Two fresh halves of an apple, the poet said.

It is midafternoon, the hour when I should be riding along on that restful comet, the daily afternoon cocktail party, with its tail of lights and ladies, of glasses and laughter, enjoying what we shall call my minor literary glory. Or rather, the glory I deserve, the glory I have a right to. One has worked, written a few books, a few articles, a few incidental pieces. One has been patient and persevering. One should now be reaping the harvest: smiles, congratulations, compliments, the false, wet kiss of glory, the poisoned cup of fame, the malicious peck of popularity. One has been stupidly wasting one's time and one's life fabricating printed rectangles of varying thickness, none weightier than a box of cigars. One might as well spend the rest of one's life giving out cigars and receiving them.

To hell with everything.

❡ 96

I am here, in the middle of the street, in winter, as dusk is descending on the city, far from the deplorable golden galaxy that is one's rightful milieu, seeing a roundness live. I buy myself a paper bag of roasted chestnuts, and the piece of newspaper grows warm in my hands from the heat of the chestnuts, and the mendacious, no longer newsworthy lines of type come to life again, giving off the smell of printer's ink, which when all is said and done is the smell of my life, of my work, but the roasted chestnuts have the smell of my childhood, which is my only truth.

I eat the chestnuts and I am happy that they are not rotten or dried up. I eat the chestnuts and walk behind the roundness, and one after the other the young girl and I—I try to make sure she doesn't notice me—walk through department stores and shops, up flights of stairs, through subway stations, streets, cafeterias. I merely want to catch one more glimpse of the wonder of an adolescence that is rounding itself off and singing, the tough, vigorous roundness, that unnecessary luxury of life that the body of a woman, of a young girl, represents, that pointless curvature—disturbing because it is gratuitous—that the creature suddenly has, an adornment, a handle that nature has bestowed on her and that serves no purpose, that doesn't contribute to the progress of the human species or to the buying and selling of material goods, but that nonetheless continues to be one of the few certain truths that I observe in the midst of the nonsensical business of living. I raise the paper bag of chestnuts high as I sometimes raise the golden loaf of bread, high in the blue day. Magritte, a Surrealist, a modest man and a genius, a Belgian and a visionary, painted loaves of bread flying through the blue sky.

I feel like a Magritte, a Magritte figure, a Magritte painting, when I make my way through noontime with my loaf of bread, as if carrying a lance of working-class gold so as to mount an attack on the gules of the sky. I live within a Magritte painting and I am the neighbor walking past; I spy on myself in the shop windows, and the bread that I am carrying is my tie to the bread I used to buy in my childhood, because the bread is the same, and once again I become that child who was sent out to run errands. Instead of the literary glory of midday, I buy bread and walk along the street with it, as one walks about with a folded newspaper, because the loaf of bread is the newspaper of the baker's shop. Instead of the literary glory of late afternoon, I buy chestnuts and watch that roundness live, not because I have renounced anything, but because I am the man in the street, the gentleman passing by, the one I saw pass by as a child.

As a child, I used to see an unhurried and self-possessed gentleman passing by in the late afternoon, and I envied him and wanted to be him someday, and it seems now that I've come to be that gentleman, or at least I'm getting there. In other words, the secret is in attaining that detachment, that eloquence, that indifference, that ability to allow oneself to be carried along by the gentle surf of the city at dusk, just to see what happens. With a loaf of bread in my hand, putting gold on the coat of arms of midday, or with a dark jumble of chestnuts that gives off smoke in the late afternoon, I free myself of the great literary error and I watch that roundness live.

We make our way through patches of light, patches of darkness, around corners, amid people on the streets, and this double roundness, or a roundness divided in two, depending on the moment, has grace, agility, vigor, dignity, youth, optimism, joy. It is just right that her pants are red and that she has come out without a coat, despite the cold, and that the pants are tight, close-fitting. The rest is a matter of motion. Plus the immobility of sculpture that I imagine her to possess when she stops to rest. In any event, it is precisely the sort of graceful abundance that life always ought to have. That and nothing more. I wouldn't want to speak to the girl. It would surely prove disappointing, but that isn't the reason either. I've scarcely seen her face. Only the profile, at one moment or another, a Bushman's eye casting a sidelong glance out of the corner outlined with mascara. Even if she turned out to be a real dish, that would be a shame. All I want is to see two masses of life moving, singing in freedom, twins, exactly alike, harmonious, unpredictable.

At the very most, I'd do the girl's toenails. I wonder if I've ever done a woman's toenails. I can't really say. I've lived it or dreamed it, read about it or imagined it. Holding her white feet, made of a childish, wholesome material, doing something or other with those nails. Painting them, counting them, I don't know what.

Caressing her foot, the little animal, the tiny mute beast, the graceful predatory creature with its five tiny weapons. Just that and nothing more. A young girl's foot, four little toes like four sleeping children. One toe that would like to be more adult, more aggressive, a youthful toe, with a certain resemblance to the naked torso of an adolescent. The cuirass of the toenail. A young girl's foot. This girl, her haste, the moment when she disappears from my sight forever, or the moment when I cease to follow her, though I am not tired and have no reason not to go on following her. How good it feels to be far from the conventional astronomy of literary parties. How far I am from the person they think I am, the person they are waiting for, the person they know, the person they love, the person they hate. How good it feels to be far from myself, from that person that I have slowly, stupidly turned into. How quickly that roundness is disappearing in the distance, singing in red. Wandering about the city and the magic encounter with a woman were articles of faith for the Surrealists. Seeing a woman from the back is enough for me. I haven't even needed to see her from the front. How quickly that girl's behind, alive and saucy, is disappearing in the distance.

My mother used to cut my fingernails. Every once in a while, on certain afternoons, she took upon herself the intimate and delicate task of trimming my fingernails, of reducing my fierce, jagged, dirty, child's claws to the clean, short curves of cared-for human fingernails. She also used to trim my cuticle. Like the slow growth of that cuticle, I was growing within her, concealing her life, eclipsing the white half-moon of her soul, and today I am the one, the father, the mother (there are times when the father is the mother, and the mother is the father, and perfect fatherhood or motherhood requires that each share something of the nature of the other) who cuts my son's fingernails. The slow growth of the cuticle, that wild cartilage that overgrows my son's fingernails, his hands full of scratches, dark patches, rough spots, chapped places. From time to time I take them in my hands as if they were two friendly toads, I hold them tight, I wash the humus of the world off them, I cut and trim the nails. This is life, perhaps, this repetition, this familiar manicuring, this intimacy, a tenderness that goes back to the beginning of time. Who did the fingernails of that little girl from a tiny village, my mother, who was she when she did mine, and what is she like now, she who is inside me, the one who does my child's, my son's fingernails? I cut my boy's fingernails, not just for him, but to awaken her in me. There are acts, incantations, secret rites that can resurrect a dead person, make him or her live within us. Every imitation is a possession, someone has said. As we imitate the dead person, the dead person possesses us. It is the only way for him or her to return to the world. That's the only way of being a genuine spiritual medium. My mother within me is doing the fingernails of her son, who is my son. As I am no longer me, because I am her, my son is her son, because I have disappeared.

I am thus the intermediary between two beings separated in time who have never met. I am the medium who knows how to disappear once he has brought two spirits together. I have somewhere the little pair of dented scissors with which my mother trimmed my fingernails. They won't cut anymore. But that doesn't matter. Apart from the fetishism of objects, through this simple ritual of cutting a child's fingernails I have succeeded in reincarnating her in me, and reincarnating myself in my son. She and I are face to face. She and I are reunited in one corner of the home where our family lives. What am I then, who am I? I am the one who looks, I am that which looks, I am the gaze of the place where the family dwells, the awareness of the family.

I see them as things see them. As they are seen by furniture and books which, though they are different from us, are the same. They are she and I. We are him and her. I can say this in a thousand different ways. Grammar is the soul's accomplice. The soul has a vast knowledge of grammar. A task taken on with tender affection, homage paid to a child, a ritual in the shadow, and the hands of a child that want to be a wild woodland again reduced to the pink and reasonable reality of the home. I am listening to my son grow. A son is one's own childhood recaptured, the missing piece in the puzzle. What I didn't live in myself I live in him; he is what I don't remember of myself. He is the piece of my life that was missing. I am the piece of my mother that was missing.

THE child draws, writes, traces his first letters, his first numbers, and it is like the days when primitive man began to paint the rock walls of his cave. My son's calligraphy is that of a little savage (there is a lost savage in every child), and his drawings are executed with the shaky lines of a pristine depiction of the world. That's how all children draw, not only because their personality is not yet formed, but because the child still lives and has his being in the state of felicity common to the entire human species. All children resemble each other, just as the folklore of every people and every primitive culture resembles every other. We are aware that individuality is a victory or a perversion brought about by culture. The child moves within the anonymous primal ooze. Every child is an anonymous, primitive creature, not because he does what he does naively, but because his art and his writing still have their roots in the undifferentiated, arcadian, common heritage of the species, of humanity. Like craft art, like pottery-making, what the child does is nameless, unsigned, despite the fact that he signs his work clearly, with an obvious, obstinate pride in the name that he has so recently won for his very own.

A potter, an anonymous artisan, the child belongs to the great craft guild of childhood and nothing else. He has the style of a small child, the purest possible style, and in no sense is he a *naïf*, as Rousseau was not a *naïf* and never took himself to be one. Every child is a savage who misses his native tribe, who has gotten lost in the jungle of adults. The signs that my son leaves behind on paper, on his slate, that trail of lines, numbers, and letters, are not so much an imitation of adult culture as a re-creation of the world on the basis of his savage assumptions, a first eager attempt to interpret and understand that world. The 4 that my son sets down is not a 4 but the affirmation of a perspective, a living faith. For the very reason that he moves in the domain of the anonymous, of the primitive and the communitarian, the child does not make signs for signs' sake; he makes them, rather, for himself, he asserts himself, he seeks to divine himself in each number, in each letter. This does not contradict the notion of anonymity and primitivism; on the contrary, it represents precisely the same phenomenon at work. Primitive art affirms collectively; behind it lies a common reason for being and a common purpose. In it is a common soul that finds expression. Only in art that is a sophisticated, adult phenomenon does the code matter more than the message. The adult makes a 4 when he needs a 4 in his calculations. When a child makes a 4, he puts his soul and his life into it. He gambles everything on each 4, the way primitive man gambled everything on each stag he hunted.

The child believes that he is learning numbers, or it may well be that he believes nothing of the sort. What he is really doing is leaving a trace of himself—a trace of a self that is still collective, childish, totally innocent—marks identifying him, facts concerning his present. Four, for a child, cannot be an abstract value. For the child the abstract does not exist. Four for the child is a chair or a stairway, not only because that makes an interesting game and because that is what the number 4 resembles, but for the simple reason that chairs and stairways exist, and 4s don't.

My son draws his 4, his alphabet, his wild animals, and all of childhood is visible once again on his slate. Something Egyptian and Etruscan and savage and palpable, the first clay of the human soul, has made its appearance. He embraces primitive animism, attributing a soul to medicines and none to himself. He is unwittingly creating Surrealism à la Vallejo, creating culture. There is no such thing as abstract thought in a pure state. What lies in the innermost depths of man is hieroglyphics, his natural handwriting by way of images, and our alphabet and our abstract numbers take on the appearance of hieroglyphs in the child's notebook, for he is in the process of carrying out, with his clumsy, persistent little hands, the tremendous cultural task of adapting one code to fit another, of cramming into our narrow abstractions all the vastness of images and forms that is the very soul of the species.

The passing days slough off my body like the flesh of lepers. The wound of time. Time is a wound, no doubt about that. I have begun to be aware of time as swiftness, to see life from beginning to end, static and complete, utterly ordinary. Yet this static quality paradoxically coincides with the sensation of swiftness, of haste. Something is drawing to a close at this very moment, but then something always is. Time. An anguish brought on by days when the sun beats down, a fruit that matures in twenty-four hours and falls, rotten, into the deep ravines of time. Nothing.

In the rainy tunnel of winter, pessimism and dampness may hold time back, make life seem longer. We then become aware of our haplessness or uselessness, and our uselessness makes us eternal. Uselessly eternal. But the moment happiness makes its appearance, the moment the light sings or the sun visibly resumes its course, time unfreezes, the great iceberg falls apart and melts away. That's when the passing days slough off my body like the flesh of lepers. They are golden pustules, entire lodes of my life, geographies of my body that I bury forever. At times one experiences the optical illusion that time is motionless, and is thus confronted with the phenomenon or the mirage of circularity. One day turns out to be like another, whereupon one experiences the torment of being hemmed in by the circumference. On the other hand, time stands still and there is nothing dragging us inexorably toward our death.

In one of these endless circles of time, the writer sometimes makes his appearance, a thread unraveling from the literary life that is at once remote and close at hand, a slippery character who has never been a faithful companion to the very end in any endeavor. He comes forth from his depths of dank erudition and homosexual passions, he emerges from his literary lair with green mold on his teeth and dandruff scales in his hair. He brings with him his soul of smelly tobacco, his smile of an elderly child, his eyes of a Chinese mandarin, his failure, his obsequiousness, his miserable rumpled elegance, and emanates an air of hatred and flattery, love and failure, resentment and melancholy, a sour aggressiveness and a sodden, unnecessary adulation. I don't care to have anything to do with him, but I listen to him, I see him making his way, doggedly pursuing the path laid out for him by his frustration, digging his own tunnels ever deeper, the tunnels that lead to his grave, returning to the rotted trunk of the tree from which he has emerged to pay me this smiling, sick visit. He is one among thousands. The literary compost heap is full of them. Single-minded madmen, envious men reeking of cologne, nearsighted dwarfs, all manner of men, the innumerable guises of frustration, because frustration can also take the form of a dull, wilfully pursued, ugly triumph. Intellectual cripples, victims of a catarrh of the soul, neurasthenics, homosexuals of learning, fools. Their number includes all sorts and types. One of them, no different from the rest, a pretentious wretch, comes to visit me and leaves on the table his puddle of erudition and slimy slaver, and goes off into the night of time, out of my light, far from my light, on which he has singed his wings for a moment, wings filthy from flying about in dirty cellars.

Then time closes in around me once again, like a ring, as I write, travel, make love, read, take leisurely walks, smile, talk with my son, and live one by one the pages of this book. The sun strips the days off my skin. The sun is like a sickness. The sun is the great sickness of the world, and the light is a relapse. I have a clear awareness that time is passing, and that is not something that one comes by easily. I have trouble sleeping, so I know that at night, too, time is passing, and I am uneasy. What you must do—and occasionally I succeed in doing—is follow the rhythm of time, because time has a rhythm, a beat, and you must not lose the beat. For a few days I manage to enter the stream, to allow myself to be carried along. It is a peaceful, pleasant feeling.

On a trip to the provinces, on an excursion out into the world, on an outing in the countryside, I gaze at the dead space of train stations, the gap, the uninteresting empty rectangle left by a freight car that has stood on a siding for a long time. I gaze at the country roads heading toward twilight, the rock that has been stamping its gesture on the sky for centuries, flinging its hands upward in a great, frozen, pointless, grandiose gesticulation. I gaze at the flat countryside over which a shadow falls from who knows where, from the cloudless sky, a shadow like a sunspot, thus demonstrating that not everything about the sun is light, not everything that illuminates is light. I gaze at the winter sea, in the cities of the world above, the fierce pastoral labor of the foam, the way it devours life and the coastline with the patience that water possesses, I gaze at the loneliness of the sea, the silence of the rotary printing presses in sleeping newspaper buildings, the tired, dusty wings of airplanes, a star-studded expanse, I gaze at the bread broken with a victim, offices on Sunday, the astonishing metamorphoses of my hair, the countryside that has left its sad teeth in my boots, the gully of my thighs, the empty expression in women's eyes when they become aware of a hollow in their flesh, I gaze at books getting dustier and dustier on the shelves, their print blurring as I leaf through them in bookstores where I am not going to buy anything, or that unexpected sunny day when winter clothes become pointless, the damp abandon with which such a day awaits us, wastebaskets full of papers and old typewriter ribbons, the toys on the top shelf of the closet that my son can't see and will never ask for, the docile obedience of doors, the brown serpent of our interminable defecations, the blue color of certain friezes that no artist has equaled since, deserted towns, with an abandoned palace like a boat that has capsized in the air, through whose overturned hull there pass sunbeam-fish and atmospheric tides. None of this is time, but merely the passage of time. I gaze at the descent of elevators, the awakening of kitchens, where last night's dinner has taken on the appearance of a crime, dogs that look at me with peaceful, self-absorbed eyes as they shit on the sidewalk, newspaper stands redolent with current events, the mysterious breakfasts of elderly ladies, grass growing before my eyes in the morning light, the keys of my typewriter, like a rough-hewn harmonium, the steam rising from the midday meal, the dreary color of faded cloth that four o'clock in the afternoon has, the death throes of cities as night falls, as an old man kills an old woman without anybody discovering the crime until the following day. I gaze at my age in the mirrors of shops, my son's slumber, the rain slanting past car headlights that have inadvertently been left on, streaks of oil on the pavement, and none of that is time.

FEVER, that secret fire that my mother anxiously searched for in herself, that she searched for in me, as later I searched for it in myself, as I search for it now in my son.

Fever, the quiet flame fanning out through the blood, that fear that frightens me as nothing else does, the consuming of the body and life in a slow, silent fire. Fever, why fever, from where, its dusky inner flames spreading to the eyes, torturing the temples, making the hands crackle?

My son's fever, the fire in which he burns me, the non-existent bonfire that consumes him, the red abyss in which I lose him. Fever and horror. How can one live amid horror? One can. Surrounded by death on all sides, the fever waving its tired banner, fear. One can live—in the midst of horror—and that's hideous. Even horror can come to be comfortable. To be in the throes of death is to be fixed, like a star, safe and sound, free of all danger, beyond all of life's flash floods.

We go out one day to buy a lamp, we have to buy a lamp, and we come home with a fever, with illness, with fear. The things that life is made of. Getting out of the house for a while, buying a lamp. All the things that I see now, in the middle of the night, lying in bed wide awake, my eyes staring into the darkness. A person unable to sleep takes his own life by surprise, he follows the subterranean course of his existence, he descends to the secret corridors of being, he looks at the light of being alive from the camera obscura of insomnia, he sees days from the perspective of night, he looks at life from the perspective of death. Everything is laid out before my eyes now, my son's fever, the comfortable aspect of horror, all the things that are happening to us, and my life is nothing but a horizontal line disappearing in the distance. I am simply a pair of eyes contemplating time. The lamp, buying a lamp, every once in a while we need another lamp in the house, and we go out shopping, we go into department stores, we search for the best of all possible lamps, we talk with sales-girls, department heads, various people as we wander through the labyrinthine cathedrals of shops and stores, undoing the gordian knot of canned music, soft indirect lighting, price tags, and the menstrual smile of the cashier, and we return home with the lamp. The lamp is there in its place now, bright and new and gleaming, creating the illusion that we are about to enjoy a light easily come by, a light that will cast its peaceful, warm glow on our life. Replacing a lamp is like putting new oil in an old lamp, as the ancients did. The house takes on a different look, we all see each other in a different light, a different color, with smiles that suddenly seem hollow and dehumanized in the glare of this lamp that is too new.

The lamp that has been turned off is turned on again in my insomnia. The house has taken on a new dimension with the new light, but we will soon feel at home in these strange regions illuminated by the lamp, and everything will be nor-mal again, the same everyday reality as always, under the lamp. It is as if this different light, like a sunny day, is pro-tecting us against something. Life continually dims lamps, continually snuffs out brightly glowing lights. My house is a new lamp and my son has a fever. My life is light and death. Shadow and life. The lamp.

We have placed a lamp in the heart of terror. The child, children. All of them are my children. To have been a father once is to have been one and to continue to be one *in saecula saeculorum*. It is at once glorious and horrifying that all of them are my children, that all of them are tortured by life under my reign as their father. All children are the same child. When one suffers, all of them suffer. Just as my child is the child of mankind, I am the father of all children and they kill them on me, they take them away from me, they burn them to death on me.

A child is a lamp of life. A child is oil whose flame can-

℃ 109

not be extinguished. How the candle of his life, the oil of his laughter, burns and throws out sparks in the fire of fever. A child is a little lamp. Children of light in the circle of light cast by the lamp. Light of a child, flesh of a lamp. Light is the body of the lamp. Children are lamps of life. Replacing the lamp, buying a lamp. And fire, fear, insomnia, terror, the child, fever, fear. Lying alone in the darkness, I see my life as a story of clouds. Nothing exists, nothing has ever existed, and I write it all so that it may somehow exist. If I get out of bed, if I take a drink of water, if I turn on the lamp, if I look around me, if I profane the light, I am party to the secret, nocturnal destruction of things.

Water in my mouth: repellent. Blood in my mouth. The sheets, warm from my body, ice-cold from the night. I turn the lamp off, and beneath my closed eyelids my eyes are open. Beneath my closed eyes my gaze is open. Beneath my closed gaze my soul is open. Something keeps looking from within me even when I am no longer looking. When there is no longer anything, it still looks within me. The night, fear, the child, fever, the lamp. It is possible to live in terror indefinitely. It is possible.

The immense looms of literature stretch out before me when I read or write. The only salvation, a feverish task. I am the shuttle and the thread, the eye that watches and the hand that weaves. I am turned into an instrument, a métier, a task. I weave a tapestry of life, because death does not deserve life and we must not give it exclusive dominion over it. Literature is a realm bursting with activity. Everything in it is alive because everything is dead. Cervantes and Proust will never die. They are their characters. They have never existed, therefore they will never die. Literature is the realm of eternal salvation. When pain clouds over my world, language is more than my métier, it is my homeland. Language, literature, what I write and what I read, what writes me and what reads me. I read the classics in the same way they read me. They read the man I am now, they interpret him, illuminate him, as I read them. They learn from me and take on a new dimension thanks to my reading of them. The torrent of thought, of culture, is a river into which I can plunge whenever the mood strikes me, in which I can drown myself in order to save myself. No one ever bathes twice in the same river of words. Languages never cease to flow. I return to them when life's fires grow too hot. I cool myself in them and sing. I have a soul in need of purification that is drawn to them. To read and to write are one and the same thing. To do either is to enter the turning wheel that becomes a gushing spring, the spring that becomes a landscape, the landscape that becomes a book. Something that comes from a very long way away, that existed long before me, and that will continue to flow after I die.

I thus inhabit the continuity of culture, the circle that is the usual pattern of the infinite. It is better to be no one in the world of culture, just another bee in the immense hive of words, a nameless weaver working at the looms of language. The great riverbed of an entire language has passed through me, with its classics, its primitives, its anonymous craftsmen, its poets. To work in the realm of literature is to work in an immortal mill. To come into contact with the dazzlingly bright cutting edge of the eternal. It is not their moral sense, we now realize, or their pretentious truths pretentiously set forth, that make literature and thought immortal, but rather that more profound morality that structure, continuity, work represent. The eternity of language is functional; it is continuity. It is perennially creating itself and destroying itself. There are as many languages as there are seas. I work within language and language works within me. It is not an illusion of eternity but something simpler, a rendezvous with continuity.

OR else I go out into the street, in the quiet of the day, and the present is a new leaf on a tree, in chilly sunlight, and the day is bright and shining, but pain burns at its center, throbs in its vitals. Tender leaf of heaven, presage of spring, joyous Sunday frost, life, mortal and pink. It is the budding freshness of a story, the morning wind, still blowing through the world in search of something, that later on, in the afternoon, tired and dispirited, will give up the search.

In the afternoon, or as night falls, pure and clear, I talk to myself on the street, converse aloud with my life, come and go, and the person that speaks from within me is not my ordinary everyday self. Rather, a foul-mouthed ragamuffin inside me pops up in this dialogue of a madman, a pariah sings, the nameless street loafer imprisoned within me frees himself, curses, blasphemes, swears like a trooper, laughs, cries, spits.

Speaking not only to set forth sententious truths, but to take the wretched boor, the madman that one is, the youngster that one was, crying out his fear and his rage in the gloom as night fell. My "inner multitudes" speak in me, take the words out of each other's mouths, whereupon I go back home, liberated and silent, as if I had left behind in the streets that entire mob that I myself am in my innermost depths.

Talking to myself in coarse, crude, basic words, taking out fragments of my inner ruins, strolling about with a sliver of feldspar from my subconscious, petrified words, and bits of verbal wood in my hand. Roots and mosses. Gangs of street urchins, boisterous bums come to the surface when I talk to myself. I don't talk to myself because I hope to speak to God someday, nor because I hope to hear God speak, since he is always silent, nor because I hope thereby to find God amid the fog. I do so as if I were opening up attics, airing out trunks, letting all the slime of obscenities and rancors that is life itself flow freely. Talking to myself, whistling, singing, weeping, as I go down the black streets of a city, just after darkness has fallen. Something I've done many times in my life. A pariah with his hands in his pockets and the pockets empty. Not a metaphysical solitude, but the stroll that the neighborhood takes around itself. Then back home again.

But my little boy is sacred. Life becomes a sacred thing in children, it has its one and only heavenly moment in the golden flesh of my son. There is an accumulation of purity, a meeting of time and the immediate present in the child's naked body, in his naked life, a decantation of light and language, and therefore life is a sacrilege when it profanes the child, when it attacks him. Life is stupid and suicidal when it vents its fury on a child, it denies its own nature, and the sickness of children has all the horror of a profanation. A sick child is a blasphemy that life utters. Through the sickness of children we discover that "life is neither noble, nor good, nor sacred." We discover the side of life that is a blind predatory animal, feeding on itself. Nearly all the movements of the universe are stupid and senseless, and an attack on the life of a child is a destruction of the one thing that is sacred. Biology is blasphemous by nature. The sanctity of the child is a light that shines miraculously in the universe, yet the primordial slime inevitably ends up having its horrible last word to say against life. A sick child is the visible manifestation of the continual suicide of the species. More than a crime, it is a profanation, and all that remains afterward is mere vegetative routine, since every possibility of man's ascent to his own true self has been eliminated.

BEYOND that is horror, the very pinnacle of horror, "so high up that nothing stirs." For at the summit of horror, as on all summits, there is absolute stillness, and it is necessary to reach the very height of horror to know that deadly stillness, that completely neutral calm that I have known, that inverse plenitude where nothing moves, nothing doubts, nothing sings, where the heart is but a bare stone and thought a silent film.

From the other side of things, in the midst of the unreality that has left a blank margin around time, I move about, I talk to my son, I write, I go out for a walk, I buy bread, and life, deprived of its leaven of days, is a form of frightful actuality, a terrible vividness of detail devoid of atmosphere. Total actuality, timelessness, a full life, but all in a mirror, movements without music and words without fragrance. Only utter pain and utter pleasure enable us to escape time, to dwell in the dead-still waters of a pool where hours don't exist. But pleasure, like pain, is tolerable whenever horror (the limit of both, though it is neither) is prolonged indefinitely, thus giving us the one eternity possible. One is eternal only amid horror.

It is true that truces make life livable, that all we have are truces, but once in a while one of these truces swells to enormous size, floods everything in the most monstrous way, and suddenly becomes the whole of life. I have the same life as ever, I live each day as I always have, I take my usual long roundabout path that leads me from dawn to dark, but it is like those times when, on finding ourselves in the presence of an animal that is watching us closely, we warily try to behave naturally so as not to startle it. Something is keeping a sharp, greedy eye on us, and I do my best to see that we act as we always do so that it will ignore us. Our life is the same as always, except that now it is a life being spied on by horror.

My little boy and colors. The other day he sat down to paint on a piece of paper pinned to his slate, and I stood there observing the natural, spontaneous, original way in which the child goes about obtaining his color effects. The child artist has no inhibitions. He paints and that's all there is to it. "If the sun doubted for a moment, its light would be extinguished," William Blake wrote. Children are little suns because they do not doubt for a moment. My son sits down in front of the paper without the faintest idea that there are centuries of painting behind him. He is unaware of the sheer weight of culture. He has just invented a particular gesture, a particular movement of his hand, a particular way of painting. He has just invented painting.

His serenity, his lack of hesitation, his certainty is amazing. He paints, he colors, he draws, he wets the brush now and then, he moves it lightly and freely over the paper. What he is doing doesn't matter, nor does it matter whether he is doing it well or badly. What matters is the marvelous freedom of the child, the mental agility that permits him to take possession of the world effortlessly. That is the only proper way to create. Only by making oneself one of these children does one enter the kingdom of artistic creation. This has been said many times, but it is a wonderful thing to see, to live. The child paints as he makes music or counts, neither hastily nor hesitantly (there is no haste or hesitancy in anything a child does, only a natural rhythm). In his hands the colors—synthetic, commercial colors bought in a paint store—become brilliant, alive, authentic, strong, incandescent. Children's works represent creation without anxiety. Only the child creates, draws, paints without ever experiencing the anxiety of the creator, and above and beyond their charm this is what fascinates us about works by children: the absence of anxiety.

My little boy is now with other sick children, in the pavilion of shadows where a little human grasshopper, a broken-spirited, badly disturbed little boy, or a little girl whose body has been mangled by a car, who sleeps the sleep of an apple that has been trampled underfoot, stirs restlessly and dies. My son lies there, his fate depending on the salvation that is dripping into him drop by drop, drops of plasma, light, life. Around his silence, the pain of the people, young mothers dark as burned-out forests, men like starved birds, croaking mournfully, the bottom of the world, the empty abyss of existence, the childish, desolate truth of life.

Children who are suffering, children who are dying, mothers with eyes as black as the she-wolves that make up legends, something that drips life or death. Nothing else. Pain hums in inner courtyards, women pass by with wash basins in their hands, children piss out their sadness, and the world stinks of infected wounds. I have rushed here with my son in my arms, at such speed that the two of us were sent hurtling to the very bottom of silence. It was like the visualization of our destiny. And now I have him here, still sick, looking out through death, and his glory is the pain of other children, feeble human ribbing poking through the corners of a shoddy bit of cloth.

The pure hand that is master of the art of creating colors out of nothingness, the briefly flowering lotus of childhood that paints the day with new lights, now lies wounded, with a needle inserted in its most delicate vein, in a vast iron clinic where the myriad steaming dishes of death make their way upward via slow dumbwaiters, and the blood that no longer belongs to anyone, anonymous and sacred, dreams serpent shapes beneath the cruel tears. What I still have left are the colors that the child has created, enigmatic golden hues of a universe that has no knowledge of itself.

The child and laughter. The laughter of a child. His laughter triumphs over death. When a child laughs, the world turns to foam, life grows lighter, and the sun bursts into flame. His laughter flows over things like swift-running water, makes the light ripple, brightens the day, and creates a simple continuity between living beings that nothing can destroy. Laughter is always a form of communication; it forges bonds between creatures, it washes them clean with the soap of contiguity. Adults have other languages at their disposal. For children the ultimate language is laughter.

Reaching his laughter, making contact with his laughter, provoking it or sharing it, is to enter the realm of what is most babylike in the child, what is most childlike in the baby. Laughter is the child's great language, his earliest and most profound one, and my one and only aspiration now is to find my son's laughter, to make it come pouring out, to listen to it from afar and from close by. There is one and only one way by which we can enter the secret crypt that a child is: through the latticework of his laughter.

When I was a small child literature to me was what is now known as the family romance of neurotics, the epic of the child convinced that he is a foundling or illegitimate, an ideal picture of the world, a retreat from reality. As literature took on greater reality in my life and I fulfilled myself in and through it, I came to believe that it was my weapon for taking possession of the world, the sword of my conquests. Now that half my life has been swallowed up by the pursuit of a literary career, it is again becoming for me what it was in my childhood and what it has actually been all along: my way of refusing to be in the world, my loathing for the society of adults, for their business deals, their buying and selling, their commercial transactions. I am pleased to note that I have not lived. The dream of the foundling, the family romance, has been realized, has come true for me. Thanks to literature, I have been able to remain on the sidelines of the human marketplace, and even when I seem to be touching the world with my prose, I am safe and sound and far away in the pure and simple art of writing, in the closed world that literature represents.

I have not lived, I have never been on intimate terms with tradesmen and butchers. I have prolonged my childhood throughout my life, I have safeguarded my dream, and therefore my life has not been wasted or blighted. Nothing can happen to me, because I am not in the world. The great achievement of my life is not having attained a certain professionalism in my work—whereby I might risk falling into the world once again—but having made the family romance, the dream of being a foundling, having abolished forever the second-rate reality that commerce and the marketplace represent. This was merely a plan I had in my childhood. Today I think of it as something that I have carried out successfully, a goal that I have definitely reached. I shall die without having passed through the world. I have never left the magic circle of literature. I have lived the world intensely, but literarily. Writing is merely the outward projection of an attitude and a point of view. The writer makes his way farther and farther inward.

THE terrace in this wintery spring. The terrace, frozen solid by winter, like a tall crow's nest in northern skies. The terrace: a small extra-domestic space, iron, brick, and glass. A wicker chair painted pink, like the skeleton of a dead summer. A child's bicycle, with something broken, twisted out of shape, awaiting the rust of oblivion. The flowerpots, with nothing but dry dirt in them now, trembling in the March wind, tiny round plots of uncultivated ground. Stones, china, forgotten odds and ends, a jumble of furniture. Nights have passed over all this, there is still a dead winter on the terrace, like a dull gray bird fallen from the desolate sky. An insecure stretch of rope, a hesitant line that makes the world look smaller, that crosses the landscape, a clothesline that dances in the air, precariously spanning the void and giving a domestic dimension to the firmament. The wicker armchair has a faded green corduroy cushion. The terrace is life lived in a little corner, the empty interval of a summer, the empty space of myself, the place where on summer afternoons and evenings I sat outside absorbed in a book or my inner dialogue.

My son is far away. I am here, behind the pane of glass, looking, but at the same time I am not here. The green has disappeared from the flowerpots, blown away by a mysterious mouth. The terrace is an open coffin, a precipice of days, one last remaining trace of a home that the failure of our life festoons with abandonment and dust.

My son and I play in white corridors, in white rooms, in white days without light, white days without sun, as if beyond life and death. We play white, ghostly games. My son and I are unreal, lukewarm, in the day without hours, in the light without sun, in the sky without daylight, playing in white corridors, white windows, white rooms, beyond his death and my life, alone and silent, calm in the face of what fate will bring. We go on playing still.

The cold house, the lonely rooms, a home life that has foundered, a solitude like a shipwreck, sad garments, overcoats like victims, things fallen from the ceiling or the sky, a redoubt of books and death that I wander aimlessly about in, talking to myself like a halfwit, searching for something, searching for myself, and despairing at the sight of a jacket on a chair, which fits the chair back perfectly, as if it were a mocking imitation of a person, of myself, with a wicker chest and no head. The waters of catastrophe have receded, and here I am, stepping on secret wet spots, lethal infiltrations, amid paintings, books, chairs, lamps, as if all this were the clearance sale of my life, the secondhand clothing store that a family dwelling always finally becomes, the secret sale-and-purchase contract of defeat, the dreadful junk dealing that we all come to sooner or later. I get myself a glass of water and wait.

Amid all the disorder I look at photographs of my son, the photo of a morning in the mountains, the little boy with a big cup in his hand, that breakfast, that day of days. He is looking at me over the edge of the cup, from beneath his bangs, with great, languid eyes in which life solidifies. My son naked in white summers, with foam in his soul, dashing against the windowpanes of happiness. My son in a large photograph, grave, quiet, vulnerable, serious, or that other image of him, on the terrace, backlighted, his laughter a sound that I can readily imagine, a fork in his hand, something that makes him glow, the concise résumé of life and pleasure that is, that was, so like him. Moments in a child's existence, instants of his life, flashes of my son, photos with animals, big beaks, heavy hoofs, friendly muzzles, the child in the mud enjoying life, the child disguised as something else, colors and lights, a very soft head. He is a year old perhaps, a certain majesty that children sometimes have at that age, the child sad, the child happy. Of all the laughter of children, his for me has a double bottom of sadness, a little trill of frailness, something that makes it both frightening to me and beloved. The child looking very serious in certain photos (from what depths does such seriousness well up in a child?), his head erect, his eyes dull, his cheeks quite ordinary-looking, with just a hint of his liveliness to come. My son in a window, in the morning or the afternoon light, snapshots of a life bristling with instants.

In the stillness of the photos one has a better glimpse of the mobility of his life. In the repose of these thin paper rectangles are sudden glimmers of the lightning swiftness of childhood. As I look at this series of photographs one by one, I see this creature who has been born and changed before my eyes, a succession of little boys who are my little boy; childhood is a multitude, an entire collection, a contraction. Every five or six months reveals a child who is completely different. The child is a series of children. I thought I loved just one child and I have loved many, a different one every day.

With a dull pain, moving only as much as the wound permits, I review my son's life, his images, the fireworks that flared up from his existence on every hand, the lightning flashes of the vault of heaven reflected in the metal of his childhood. A rivulet of untamed life wriggling free of life's grasp, a slithering happiness that is coming to an end now. My son.

For as long as I can remember, I have made rough sketches in my dreams of the grace of his soul, a grace without a past, and then day by day I have seen these dream molds fill up with certainty. I have explored as thoroughly as I could the new dimension that he opened up in life, like a cool mountain pass of green music. I now palpate aching flesh in my soul, and the whole of my existence is taking its course inside a gaping wound. The one unheard-of possibility of life is a child. With time, he himself comes under the sway of a reality whose potential has deteriorated and becomes a man, a sterile, reasonable block of existence. The neutral, known depths of life absorb the child in the end. Childhood dissolves in its own self and disappears. Where have all our childhoods gone?

A child is a light that is snuffed out in its own smoke, a flame that blows itself out. The child one day disappears in the man. What remains of a childhood? Flotsam and jetsam: photographs, ribbons, wires. Childhood is a fragrance that vanishes as one breathes it in. Man begins his existence as nothing more than a scent.

A child invariably ends up getting lost in the forest of grownups. Perhaps that is the real meaning of stories for children. Childhood is perpetually threatened, destined to disappear forever on a dark, peopled, adult horizon. We will inevitably lose our son, in life or in death. But no one can take away from me the cool rain shower, the gust of wind, the radiant, harrowing dimension he brought to the world all of a sudden, and brought to me. A son is a flash of lightning from the future that dazzles us for a moment. Through him, through my son, I saw farther, farther inside, farther into the distance, and perhaps—oh, how it hurts to say so— that is enough.

Something that made my son glow: a fork in his hand, or his soul. His unconditional acceptance of life. As for myself, and the summing up of what has made me happy? If I draw up an inventory now, if I distill in my memory what my life has been, the light that it has given, the moments of joy, all that is but a sad drop of sunlight. What was once extreme, paroxysmal happiness has now turned to dull, disappointing gold once again. On some afternoon or other, I don't remember exactly when, on a woman's body, on the mad skiff of a morning when I was a young boy, I was happy. I see a woman's body, a snapshot of the sea, a light. Nothing.

We know that we have lost a handful of coins of happiness somewhere, that we have a little copper coin of light left, a memory. Surely it wasn't like that, either. I have buried a treasure deeply, something that is a treasure only for that reason, because it is buried. The moment I dig it up and take it out into the light again it will be nothing.

The breeze, the brightness of the day: all of a sudden something brings to mind the fragrance and the memory of paradises I am unable to identify. Music invents a past for us that is unknown to us, someone has said. Scents, spring, clouds also suddenly take us back to a past that is unknown to us. All we have of happiness is the memory: we have never experienced it in and of itself. Man knows happiness only by way of indirect references. Obscure inner references. Happiness cannot lie in the future, because it always comes to us by way of memory; it is in our memory that its image is imprinted. Happiness is something that has happened once and only once. Our memory of it is so vivid and at the same time so distant that it doubtless belongs to the past of the species. But all this becomes confused automatically, and we project what is merely a vague recollection into a hypothetical future. Happiness is unattainable precisely because it is something we remember. It has already been.

We feel instinctively that happiness is yet to come, that the word *happiness* refers to the future. It really refers to a remote past, from which we extrapolate it into the remote future through the workings of an automatic mechanism of self-defense. It has been said that science fiction is full of nostalgia for prehistoric times. This is true. One can dream only of the past. The future is a past that is taking on a potential reality once again. I am confident that I will be happy because I was happy once. I believe that I was happy once because at the time I believed, in similar fashion, that I had been happy at some time in the past. Every moment of happiness is merely the confirmation of the fact that we have a past. It is only memory that knows pleasure.

My name, my aura, and what I have created around me? The name of a writer. Anyone who feels at home within the aura of fame surrounding him ought to go out into the country, into nature, and say aloud: "I am a writer, I am important, I am . . ." I am sure that he would find himself unable to finish the sentence. All that means nothing in the mountains, at the seaside. Our renown goes no farther than the city line. We lose it in the country, or when we travel. We must arrive at another boundary line in order to find it again. I feel important in the city, in the same familiar surroundings. Places, people, newspapers, things that reflect my image. The moment I go just a few kilometers away from the heart of the city I am lost. I have lost my image. I must arrive in another city in order to recover it, in order to recover my self, in order for other newspapers, other people, other mirrors to reflect me. Celebrity, fame, popularity, renown, mere prestige end just around the corner. They cannot survive a bus trip to the outskirts of the city, a train ride to the suburbs. You are important only as long as you don't budge from your usual spot. The minute you cross the street you are lost. We are anxious to get to another city so as to recover everything we have been in the process of losing as we journeyed through the vast expanses of countryside, at once so real and so alien. That's why writers don't often venture into the countryside.

Solemnity. I have given up solemnity. In the final analysis the one aim of our struggle in the world of letters is to win the right to be solemn. We don't do battle in order to become profound, truthful, useful, or better persons. We fight for the right to become solemn. I never believed in my own solemnity, I have no doubts on that score, but suddenly, lo and behold, one finds that one has earned the right to be solemn. The moment would seem to have arrived when it is incumbent upon one to don the proper facial expression and the proper clothes, to carry oneself as straight as a ramrod, and to speak in a firm voice at all times. At the age of forty, if one has worked industriously and not done too many crazy things, if one has lost one's life by being overly polite—as Rimbaud lamented—one can now be solemn.

I have earned that right. I have written a number of books, I have made a name for myself, I have given out autographs. The moment of solemnity would appear to have arrived. Now that I have the right to be solemn, I don't want to be.

On certain mornings I try to be. I stand in front of the mirror, imagining myself dressed solemnly, going out onto the street with the monocle of fearless impertinence, the top hat of respectability, the elegant inquisitive cane of age, hypothetical full-dress gloves. Solemn. Then I inevitably go back to corduroy, leather, boots, wool, open-necked shirts, old clothes. I know that inside me is a solemn man, as there is inside every writer, every politician, every intellectual. The solemn man within me has tried to make his appearance at one moment or another, to dominate the situation, to choose homburgs edged with fine ribbon. In time, he has always gone back to where he came from. Within me there is also a street urchin who has whistled mockingly at him.

I see the solemn men around me, my colleagues, aged by their solemnity, at once self-satisfied and insecure, like presidents of themselves, and I realize that at this late date I shall not manage to become solemn, that I shall never know what it is to look the part, as the saying goes, to wear my name, my prestige, properly. Alas.

On the contrary, I would like to earn oblivion. Not unjust oblivion, of course, since that is simply another form of fame, not a pantheonlike oblivion. Just a modest little oblivion—living forevermore in the enigmatic crypt of a name seldom visited, being, when tomorrow comes, a dead man with no marks of identity. Almost everyone who writes wants to linger on in people's memory in the form of a municipal statue, a public square that bears his name, a savior of the country. Civic glory and that of textbooks are to be avoided at all costs. One must fight against being turned into a useful lesson. The best way to do so, I think, is to create scandal. However scandalous a figure the writer, the artist, may have been, however much of a troublemaker he may have appeared to be to his contemporaries, he is immediately taken up again by the next generation, made use of, taxidermized for the benefit of posterity. He is sanitized, turned into an exemplary model for youngsters studying prosody or ethics. There are numerous important instances of the workings of this process. In point of fact it constitutes the entire history of culture. The transvaluation of all values, as Nietzsche was to say, but taken to mean precisely the opposite of what he intended. What was subversive in its day becomes instructive with time. Culture is a process of domestication.

No, it is pointless to defend oneself by creating scandal or rebelling. In the end they turn you to good use anyway. In the end they cast you in bronze, which is what they want. Oblivion is better. Not a grandiose oblivion, a pantheonlike injustice, a beyond from which one returns one day with the solemnity and the laurel wreath of the dead. No. A modest little oblivion. Lingering on, not as a statue or a beacon of culture, but as an enigma, as a name that vaguely rings a bell, that means something, though no one is quite sure what, as someone that nobody has really read, and that a young girl, a student, discovers one day on a library shelf among other tomes turned yellow with age. But this should not be the discovery of her life, nor should she fall in love with the dead man. No. Just a little discovery that leads her to say, as she pushes her bangs out of her eyes in order to read what I am now writing: "That man wasn't a bad writer. What he had to say was interesting. He must not have written very much. Too bad." That's all. May she turn the page and that be the end of it. May she believe that I wrote little, and forget me.

There is always a girl, somewhere in the world, who is

writing something about me, about my books, even though she herself doesn't really know why. I am pleased at the idea that I am an intimate part of her private life, that my books and her underwear are jumbled together in messy dresser drawers, that she deposits on my pages the breath of her life and the fatigue of her sleepless nights spent pondering my words. She has chosen me by sheer chance. It means nothing. Maybe she has chosen me because I am unknown, because I am rare. That's what I would like to be, rare, a copy hard to find, an incunabulum, an anonymous work.

The girl works on what I have worked on. She is insatiable; by letter or in person, she asks me endless questions that I am unable to answer. She wants to know things about me that I myself don't know, she forces me to ponder the reasons behind my own work, which seems to me fortuitous, sporadic, capricious, and lacking deliberate plan, and which her faith turns into something systematized, consistent, continually evolving, and responsible. The girl student writing a thesis is like a gardener coming round to care for, to bring back to life, a garden long forgotten and abandoned. How do I tell her that I never stroll through this garden these days, that I couldn't care less about it? Her faith has saved it, her faith has saved her. But there is no one to save me.

The theses, the translations, the papers that try to turn one into a closed, exemplary system—I can't imagine what they'll do in my case. I hope that the translations, which I never read, are full of murky passages that lend a certain Surrealist and Dadaist air to what I have written, which is undoubtedly all too clear, suspiciously clear. It pleases me to have arrived at this chaste intimacy with the girl who is working on my books. They doubtless already smell of her, of her perfume, of her hair. The rest doesn't matter. I cannot add anything to her, or she to me. Culture is a closed circle.

It does matter, on the other hand, it is important to me to know that a woman is busy hemming, tatting, crocheting with what I have written, with what I have lived, with my life and my work, delving into them with respect and genuine curiosity. Yet she reproaches me for never speaking of God. God is indeed a problem.

I sometimes need God to blame him for my son's suffering. Is this a form of faith? Gods live in large measure on the indignation of men. Indignation overcome, accepted, sublimated, is faith. Thus far I have not needed God to feel despair. This would be a shabby use of God. But humanity knows no other.

Over a lifetime, nearly everyone has had something supernatural happen to him. I never have. Not a single ghost, not a single apparition, not a single premonition, nothing. I have always tried to expose myself to magic drafts, to be at the exact spot where secret paths meet. But no mysterious wind has ever caught me up and carried me away. Who has not felt his heart pound inexplicably, who has not seen ghosts on a rainy night, who has not breathed the smell of death in the cellar of his house? I've never had anything of the sort happen to me.

I am always favorably disposed toward trances, prepared for levitation, ready for miracles. I hope to see a phantom in every corner, I look for one in all the rooms of the house, I court mystery in long hallways, peek under the beds for it. Never a live dead person or an apparition, never a ghost from the past or strains of music from the beyond. I am unbearably earthly. Everything that happens to me could happen to anyone. How long must I wait for mystery to enter my life?

Clearly I am not a good conductor of cosmic electricity. I am surrounded by the *cordon sanitaire* of my petty skepticism, in no way prepared for the unknown. The only things that have happened in my life are real things, sometimes terrible, sometimes pleasant, sometimes bloody. None of the things that happen to other people. No dreams, no visions. I won't even bring up the word *mysticism*. Or the word *parapsychology*. I'm a miserable failure. My life has always been opaque, and I have used what lyrical talents I possess to make it shine with a light other than its own.

I flee at times, I willingly admit, to that tranquil, fictitious world, to that life that is at once possible and nonexistent, thereby escaping from my own life, from this shipwreck in which no one drowns, from this disorder of paintings that must be hung, books that must be read, things that ought to be written, with death passing through everything, lights, time, my son, days, furniture, words, gifts, silently threading its way through life. Or else, seeking to salvage something, I draw my little boy's portrait yet again. Allow me to do so here, to sketch, in words that come easily, the innocent and artistic, overly artistic disorder of his graceful head, his kitten's nose, his eyes, petals of a dark flower, at once leaf and fruit, with their halo of profound sadness or something worse, something that frightens me so, and the quite normal expressiveness of his mouth, its exquisite contours, a mouth that sometimes crinkles to form intimate words and sometimes puffs out, at once weak and masculine, to form violent words that are nothing but foam. Those cheeks like an overripe fruit that no harvest will gather, the firm body that is so recent a thing, that I take in my arms in order to hug its simple grace, his hands, as yet only a rough sketch, or his feet, so tiny, a minuteness emerging from the delicate preliminary sketch that his body is. This child, like all children: parts of him completely formed, and others still embryonic.

APRIL. April is a footprint in the grass filled with water. April is a little girl swallowed up by stems. The slim, straight waist of young girls is related to a mysterious world of svelteness. Where do young girls come from? It cannot be that the species so readies its arms, hones its weapons to a keen edge, merely for the purpose of reproduction and fecundity. The pure root of the hair, the twin harvest of the breasts, the poplar tree of the waist, the gentle calm of the hips, the swiftness of the long legs: bodies formed for something more. Where do these feather-light, feminine hosts come from each April, what paradise do they bring with them, where are they going? A lost svelteness roaming the universe is commemorated in them. Something unknown to humanity. April, a green foam under my son's tiny feet, the feminine haunch of the world, the pale flank, a wild tongue spoken by the rain, the language of every springtime that ever was, a torrential calligraphy that leaves the simple secret of the universe written on the air. April, the thrust of light toward felicity, a greenness despite everything, a child's fist suddenly opening, full of shining things, a sea wandering about the sky. April marshals its unique green color to fight death. Simple as a boat, as a lance, as a son. April knows nothing of my pain, sways to and fro amid the fronds of death, inscribes everywhere, with an ink of just one hue, a single green, indecipherable word, and does not listen to my lament because it has no ears. April, a rain-word, a flute-word in other languages too: *Abril* in mine, a word that resounds with the echo of other words, *atriles, añiles, perejiles*—music stands, indigo dyes, sprigs of parsley. What is it that opens April?

For me, alas, it opens nothing, closes nothing.

April. (Three variations)

April, a green well full of drowned damsels weaving the linen of the depths and sighing at the moon on nights made for carnal congress. April, a bright-colored bird poisoning itself on lilies floating in celestial pools. A living willow, a joyous cypress with a skeleton inside. A piece of furniture on the roof, with cloud-mirrors, the bright gilt of dawn, and delicate scrollwork. April, an alleyway of rain giving forth the mysterious, delicate scent of a garden that no longer exists, of a severed hand, of a little girl urinating.

> *April sings,*
> *stamps its feet, grows, plays a muted violin,*
> *climbs to the top of all the adobe walls,*
> *plucks things out of the sky,*
> *bites into a green fruit*
> *and bathes in the nude,*
> *stark naked,*
> *in the ice-cold current of terror.*

April. A page written all by itself by the forest scent of the paper. An abandoned car has grass growing between its wheels. The magazine leafed through smells of comforting rain. The young girl will never know that the key to her beauty lies in that bending of the light that curves her shoulder downward and lifts her rump, and I will never know that my hair changes color as I speak, as I write, and that conflagrations follow one upon the other in my head as I think of a naked girl or make up words that coincide, only by sheer springtime circumstance, with words in the dictionary.

My little boy in the midst of little girls. Carolina, with her tense, controlled, hermetic beauty. Yolanda, with her soft spongy smile and eyes. Mariona, impenetrable as a fruit. María José, a nameless and colorless flower, as tiny and smiling as a little touch of sadness. My little boy in the midst of little girls, happy.

THE wind, the wind. The wind ever and always, in my life, on lonely nights, in some secret April, the wind, asking the house questions that it does not know how to answer, shaking it. (The girl's mind, I remember, often went completely blank, and she was very quiet when she made love, on her knees, naked, withdrawn, her eyes focused on nothing, not even somewhere far away: nonexistent.) The wind, sketching the world with a stern profile, filling the world out like a black globe. Not the pure profile of my mother, over which there passed days, suns, sorrows, fevers, hours, children, lights, fears. No. The immense, grim profile of the wind, that beyond toward which it drives all things before it, that crack of death it blows them into. (The girl, as I say, was simply not there when she made love.) The wind, a vessel that founders in the night, an evil banner filling all absences, the voice of no one filling the world. The wind, as in a child's fears, bringing those fears and that child back to me once again. Searching the house, turning it upside-down in a revolution that will cease at dawn, blowing across my sleep as if across a quiet lake. The wind, drawing up a gloomy résumé of life, of death, of the present and the past, summoning forth a general catastrophe that is itself, and taking its leave howling, only to return again the very next moment. The house continues to shake even though the wind has stopped blowing, and then the wind immediately takes hold of it once again and sets it shaking even more violently. Wind worse than lightning, thunder, fire. The one thing that has terrified me is wind, that empty sea that it hurls down upon us, that disaster that it carries from one end of the world to the other. The wind, full of moaning mothers. My entire biography demolished by the wind, and I myself lying in the wind, naked, cowering in fear, all alone, shipwrecked by the arid gale-force winds.

Wheels and sorrows descend, life separates from itself, dissolves, from within we watch ourselves living the process of living itself, this pain that goes so deep divides me in two, like a scimitar, and the springtime around me stages its battle of colors, expresses itself in yellows, mauves, greens, creating a splendor and a paradise that—as I realize today—absolutely no one on the planet possesses.

What a painful month of natural bonfires, what an oppressive waste of unbreathed beauty. My son and I set fire to the dark detritus of winter together, we make lifeless flames leap forth from the black sewer of the world and walk about amid the springtime enveloped in the smoke of the ultimate dung heap, strolling through the blind fire of death. The funereal scent of all the flowers penetrates us and sometimes I take my son in my arms, beneath a sky from another, happier time, or I hold him by the hand, allowing his tiny footsteps to learn the world and its steep slopes plunging downward.

Skies, pine needles fall, and we enter the intimate shadow of a pine tree as if it were a religious grotto, or we skirt the multitude of flowers in search of an eternal day that is simply the sum of all days and that, alas, is no longer within our reach. My son, my son. The spring is a bridal wreath, April and May are flowers tucked into the locks of an adolescent girl, into the green hair of the world's puberty. We pass from sunlight to shadow, as from life to death. We pass from life to death, from death to life, as from sunlight to shadow and back again, and this game is living, and the saving grace of spring doesn't save us from anything, because spring itself is threatened with death.

My son and I. We light fires, bonfires, like two lonely hobos wandering through the city dump, and stamp on the flames joyously, desperately, he with his incredibly soft, weightless little foot, I with my huge, weary, black foot. The two of us are what is very big and what is very small, life's fateful extremes. We are unable to arrive at that middle term that would save us. The little boy picks up a pine cone and puts it in his pocket to keep.

I have taken my little boy to the sea, as I have at other times, in the hope that its health of iron and sunshine may prove contagious. The sea, a serpent that slithers about the planet, hisses in the night, and shows its gleaming steel scales in the daytime. I have run along a beach that stretched as far as dawn, along that edge of the world where the sharp pains of living scarcely ever reach, and where the vagueness of the ages begins.

The sea offers itself to children. Much effort, much painful toil, much time are required for a man's hand to take something from the sea. The child puts his hand into the water and takes out a little crab, a gleaming shell, something. One must not defy the sea, as fishermen and sailors, admirals and whalers do. One must enter it with a feeling of trust, of security, the way a child does. The sea is the terra firma of children.

I want the sea to sweep away all my pain and all my time in a single huge wave. That is precisely what it does. Then pain and time return, but they are familiar experiences now, experiences I feel at home with. The sea is never disappointing. An adult sky, a young sea, an earth of light. The rhythm of my thighs as I run through the sand, through the water, silent pistons that have tirelessly propelled my life. The wind and the water create an unknown new being that approaches my face and looks my body over. My son, a friend of the sea, has his little interchange with the monster every morning. From this commerce with the sea, the little boy brings back sea urchins, shells like mermaids' breasts, roots, treasures of sand, gold and silver of land and sea. A wave gives the one milligram of silver that it contains only to a child.

The sea is a monument to freedom, the only possible statue of liberty. The sea is a statue that has fallen down. The child, an outlander in life, is immediately adopted by the sea, the blue-and-green school of all childhood. I leave my son at the seashore, more sure of the sea than of men. The two of them recognize each other instantly.

To cut through life, that pulp of light in the air like the flesh of a fruit, to enter May as if it were a towering wave, one's lance set firmly in its socket, to die and to kill, a vague cannibalism that awakens in a man with the arrival of spring, to consummate a woman, a crime, a pleasure, a pain, a catastrophe. So much suffocating beauty, the asphyxia of living, the eroticism of living, an erotic illumination suffusing the sky above and the earth below. Fear of myself, of that cruel and poetic, implacable and violent creature that peers out from mirrors when mirrors have the black light of day behind them. Inner experience, sexual experience, illumination, May is a fleshy pulp of blood and sun that the primal horde that I am seeks to enter by way of blood and fire, sex and fire. Beneath the sky, an immense, serene wound of unquenchable light, I am stopped dead in my tracks by the pain that I feel for my son, and I see the huge blue rent in the firmament, edged in fire. The sky is burned earth, a day and a night are burning up there, and we terrestrial beings are here below, under the conflagration, with a son sleeping in our arms or a woman inlaid like a mosaic on our breast.

So I return to darkness, I close the door on the subtle fragrances of spring, I block up the narrow breaches through which the light enters with an apple of shadow, and look at my son's chair, his little straw-bottomed chair, at once unimaginable and utterly real, an object perfectly suited to his tender years, just the right size for his terrible weariness. If he were not around—what a heartbreaking thought—to sit in it, if he were to disappear from my life, what would this chair be like?

The chair would be his very self. The chair would be my son, and the empty place left by his absence would have the same curved shape that it now has, and I would love a chair as I love a child, and the only thing left would be his chair. His very own chair forever and always, to contain and convey his absence. The chair would be sacred.

The slate, the little elephant with the upraised trunk and the round yellow belly. The soft little red elephant, the slate on which my son writes with the chalk of innocence numbers that are like stairs and letters that are like mutilated butterflies. How he makes everything that is his an intimate part of himself, how deeply he penetrates his world, how unquestionably it belongs to him. It is only the child who has the ability to truly possess anything. Later on, when we are grown up, things become detached from us, they are ours only through vulgar monetary transactions, rape, legal possession, hoarding, the drive to collect things; they are property, and property is crime. Everything belongs to a child naturally, especially what immediately turns into his very image and likeness, what immediately resembles him. How much a slate, a cloth elephant, a little straw-bottomed chair resemble him. Childhood is the miraculous age in which everything we touch begins to resemble us and becomes part of us. The child, like God, creates the world in his own image and likeness. I look at the things that are my son's without his being there as I would look upon the world without man. There outside is the freedom of May, the luminous catastrophe of the sky, woman's continual metamorphoses, a golden flock of self-created forms. Here before me is the world of my son, silent and alive, infinitely fragile and full of pain. Nothing torments me so much as the beauty of the world. We make our way toward death amid a sumptuous calamity, a mortal spring. A magnificent massacre awaits us—prepared by whom? By no one. Man dies surrounded by beauty, amid the splendor of summer or the chill palaces of winter.

The world: a living pantheon, an incomparably beautiful pyramid, a burning pyre of corpses whose flames scorch the sky. Each star is the tip of a flame that has left its trace in the firmament. Death embellishes the world, death touches the immense heights with its light and the tininess of my son with its awesome tremor. We are born and die between two fires of surpassing beauty. Man is merely the momentary witness of all this gratuitous beauty.

My son's chair, all by itself, empty.

We must bury our snouts in pain, drink it straight from the source, as one drinks from springs with the taste of iron. Let this flesh of light soak up all the shadow. We must drain to the very bottom the overflowing pond of blood. We must drink evil, suffering, down to the last drop, not in little sips, not in faint-hearted swallows, but in long, deep drafts, where-upon it becomes a neutral fire, a nothingness, and the one thing that remains in the end is the simple earthenware container of life. I journey to the end of my pain, I go all the way, I drink of myself, I quench a thirst for suffering that was within me without my knowing it. The satiety of pain is like the satiety of pleasure. The threshold of an empty peace, of a sky without depth or color, of a neutrality of climate and flesh that is nothing less than the devastating impartiality of nature.

Happiness is a shorter path. Pain is a labyrinth that brings with it the fear that we will be lost in it. Happiness takes us in a straight line, and this is something worth more than happiness itself. Pain is assailed by constant doubts, it keeps blindly retracing its steps, like a sullen wild animal trying over and over again to master the path it learned long ago. I follow its dim hoofprints and every so often, I confess, I drink of bitter stagnant waters that taste of iron and death. I don't flee from my pain, I don't measure it out in careful doses, like the cautious suicide or the lady suffering from insomnia. I drink and drink. The poison will strike me dead or I will drain it to the very last drop. I don't want my suffering to come in little silver spoonfuls. I bury my snout in it and drink it straight: the gushing blood of a child, the death of a child, the sweetish, stubborn, stupid hemorrhaging of the world.

ON nights of great anguish, at the foot of my sick son's bed, watching his pain-racked journey toward death, I felt the deep pull of childhood, long ago and far away, the return to a time when nothing had happened, to the beginning of my life. Searching for the consoling and enlightening simplicity of my early years, I wrote the following:

A street studded with stars, a little corner of time, a world so small I could measure the size of it with a string. Morning gold impoverishing the sky, suns made of an eternal brick every afternoon. From the countries of dawn came peddlers, with a dead man floating in their shrill cries as they hawked their wares. Street of pitch-black night, a mythology of fear, mothers of the dead in the mud walls of January. The immense churches rang with silence and the gigantic mare of time immemorial passed by. The man at the farthest remove from myself was a milkman and the God of infinite space was my grandfather.

I wrote by the light of a pocket flashlight, by the light of a drop of water, by the light of the night, a dirty sheet of paper on my knees, seeking the comforting assonance of a simple bit of prose or a few lines of poetry. That is how I came up with things like the passage below, things that I copy here in this journal for the very reason that they lack all literary value (on the sheets of paper that I originally wrote them on, they are surrounded by the simple, pridefully exaggerated sketches that I drew of my son's face):

To go back again to the child you once were, I don't remember exactly when, to climb up to the familiar sky of the bell tower once again: on afternoons in May the sky was an attic, with suns wandering through it and birds dying in it. To have lived nothing of what has happened to me, but instead, through my son, to die somewhere in my own neighborhood. A neighborhood of dim lights, a sailing vessel that had broken up, when my aerial map showed nothing. Not to have taken this pointless roundabout autobiographical path only to return to the time of miracle a dead man. I am watching over a child who is myself, an ecstatic self.

The comforting rhythm of the short lyric poem in Spanish. What a path of light for the return to simplicity. The Spanish language and the short lyric poem are a way back that can only lead us to what is simplest and most secret in our lives. So at that time I wrote, with that lapidary insight that comes in the bad moments: suicide is the only valid answer. All the rest—art, culture, the life of the mind, politics, philosophy, religion—is nothing but fake answers, postponed suicides.

I have known the only possible truth: my son's life and death, the latter a truth I lived intensely before the fact. Yet I chose, or am choosing, deception, self-deception, and hence I will be a fraud forever. Don't believe a word of what I say, a word of what I write. I am a hypocrite. The mere fact of going on living makes us hypocrites. Life is evil because it is basically a fraud, a fraud we accept in order to go on living. As my son breathed a thick black wind, already blowing out of another world, I would read, by the light of a pocket flashlight, his collection of children's adventure stories, his little illustrated storybooks, and I could smell the woodsy odor of the printer's ink—tales of trappers and cardsharps, of cabin boys and redskins, that enabled me to capture once again the sharp fragrance of the eternal rose of my own childhood, to flee those crudely colored worlds of comic books, that pap incapable of creating any sort of believable reality.

Ghosts, specters are real: I have seen them. The ghost is the oxygen tank wheeled to the bedside of the dying patient, that great round ball that arrives with a great iron clanking, as if it were dragging ghostly chains behind it through the corridors of the clinic in the dark of night. Then the oxygen tank remains at the foot of the bed, wrapped in a white sheet, underneath which one can see its black iron curve. Then there is the hard, sharply outlined shadow of the cypress tree of death, a sinister halbardier at the head of the bed of the person about to die. But my son has had a tiny, minimal, sweet and gentle resurrection of the flesh, a resurrection that I too am experiencing as I write, with the resignation of having gone through everything now, and the little bit of tenderness that he and I can still give each other is enough for me, because I know that life lies at the heart of death as the pit lies at the heart of a fruit, and the total fruit that the universe represents is what is now casting its orchard light on our last hours, my son.

The wheelchair. I am taking my boy somewhere in a wheelchair. Once, when he was just a baby, I wrote a piece entitled "The Rocking Chair," in which I described how I put him to sleep every night, before tucking him into his cradle or his crib, in my rocking chair where I usually sat as I read or chatted. Now there is the wheelchair. It is another peaceful journey, like the one in the rocking chair, another journey that takes us nowhere, and we go down white corridors, black corridors, by way of little eighteenth-century villages, moons like sickles, alpine snows, flowers and cats, and vague creatures smile at him as we pass by, a blank lost smile, and they address him as "little girl," because the approach of death feminizes a man—a little boy in particular—just as it sometimes masculinizes a woman, for death has no knowledge of sexes, it is frighteningly chaste, and we steal flowers from the dead—docile geraniums—in a little moment of quiet happiness, as soothing as a cough drop.

Until I realize that I am the one who is being taken somewhere by the wheelchair, that my boy is pulling me, that we are heading for an unknown precipice, that I am a corpse walking behind a wheelchair, or that I am wheeling along a tiny bit of death, a child who weighs nothing, a life that has no meaning. I would like this to go on forever, to continue to pass doors, corridors, sickly smiles of incurable invalids, I would like our journey to go on and on, son, and have you mine even like this, looking down at you from above, seeing your curly head and your tiny sick hands, like the hands of those child-mummies that sometimes come to light in the upper Nile.

And so I would like everything I write now to have the simplicity and immediacy of the intimate journal, of this journal, of what one sets down in his most candid and straightforward hand, so as to reduce to the minimum the hypocrisy of living, that is inevitably duplicated by the hypocrisy of writing. Read me simply, face to face, canceling out between the writing and the reading any formality that would distance, and therefore falsify, what I am setting down, which is neither the grand spectacle of philosophy nor the traditional narrative conventions—nothing but the writing of a man who keeps scribbling interminably in his journal in order not to die, but also in order not to live.

My son's laughter. I have lost my son's laughter. How long has it been since I last saw him smile? In this very same journal I wrote that one enters the secret crypt that a child represents only by way of the latticework of his laughter. There have been no more peals of laughter, no more smiles from my son. His seriousness of earlier days turns out to have foreshadowed this thoroughgoing seriousness, this manner of being an adult that sickness visits on a child. I kiss his belly, still round and warm, his bellybutton, and in so doing I kiss a bundle of life, a sweet parcel of blood, intestines, digestions, respiration, the ultimate, powerful, tender redoubt of his vital palpitations. The child is sacred. I know, as the poet knew, that life is not noble or good or sacred, and I find nothing to respect or worship. In heaven or on earth, there isn't a single being, not a single man, who has proved worthy of my devotion, but it is through this son that I have had and lost that there will always be for me, in light at its purest, in the splendor of what does not exist, a sacred being, a golden creature. So my son becomes a creature apart from creation, a lightning flash of the sacred never seen before in the entire universe.

The suffering of children made Dostoevski doubt his faith. Albert Camus—I don't remember whether I have noted this elsewhere in this journal—says: "I refuse to love a creation in which children are tortured." Keats, voicing a more banal thought perhaps, mistrusts the world because women are victims of cancer. A person is beatified these days because he saved the life of a little girl through a miracle. Does this God whose eye is on little girls who suffer and who saves them also have his eye on the millions of children who are victims of violence, starving, mangled, struck down by cancer, hopelessly debilitated?

Far removed from all this, reduced more or less to a vegetable, I push my son about in the wheelchair to give him a change of scene.

My son's eyes, eyes that yesterday were open flowers, night buds, today have narrowed to sad little slanting slits, nearly closed by exhaustion and mistrust. How do his eyes see us, what world does he see, through what filters of night and fear, of sleep and death, does he see this cruel world flooded with sunlight, monstrous with blood? How does he see me, a vast mountain range of tenderness? How does he see his mother, an overflowing spring of eyes? What does the child see, what world does he see, what full-blown rose did he gaze at once upon a time in the air, what sad passageway does he see now in the night?

I suffer as a man, to the limit of what it is possible for a man to suffer, with my man's resources and my man's mechanism, but within me, within this suffering, there is something that suffers even more, a flesh of sobs almost entirely submerged, an ultimate, retractile bottom of pain that I am afraid to descend to, that I dare not touch. It is now a more or less vegetable-like suffering, the moan of a flower whose stem has been broken—we know today that plants moan—a pain that is not human, a fear antedating man, a jellyfish of fear—I don't know. The most sensitive and painful area of whatever is alive, marine and vegetable cartilage, aware of nothing but pain, where something pulses endlessly, far, far below my rational, banal pain of a man who is suffering.

HE looks at the slow past, persistent as the ocean wave, he looks at the return of everything with phosphorus in its teeth, he looks at the black summer, as high overhead as a planet, when the dagger of his chest sings without hope. I mean by this that the truth of the bird is not the shattered crystal of its pure call, but the blind dripping, as silent as a pronoun, with which death turns over page after page of silence. You must be mindful then, when the mirror moans, of how perfect air is, as free-flowing as the future, and de-flower slowly, very slowly, with light between your eyes, the wild weeping creature with claws. Because the humid and mysterious time to venerate the sacred bottom of glass vessels has passed and the moment has arrived to proclaim with hatred the eternity of a transparent body trapped amid swords.

REDUCED to my fecal state, my life a precarious thing based on an assumption of feces, as I headed in death's direction by way of diarrhea, sitting on the glorious excremental dais of toilets, in contact with the intestinal quivering of the world, I placed myself in a position facing the sea, and the sea was a malevolent green insect moving two cruel, translucent wings in the sun of a miserable summer. I have thus plunged into cities drenched with sinful sweat, I have lain dying alongside perverted, copper-colored old men, in modernist cathedrals, until I returned at last, all alone, my strength gone, my legs clasped tightly together, empty-headed, to this rectangle of intimacy, the delicate stains of the house, the dust of the dead on the enormous faded paper flowers, a veil of years on the books and their multitude of letters, the simple and ingenious mechanism of a family, everything that death dismantles, leaving the pieces strewn about the floor, as in the midst of a move from one dwelling to another. That is when I wrote a letter to my wife, not because I wanted her to read it, but because I wanted to include it here, in this journal, as a testament in which nothing is bequeathed to anyone, as a written message from beyond death, which is where the two of us live and have our being now:

Beginning with those afternoons, remember, when the little city brought its sunsets to an end in a fair to middling apotheosis, down to the light of this afternoon, a light of water and the beyond, we have been plotting to produce a son for death, something tremulous born of you and of me, a scheme hatched on rainy nights and days of hard work, a brightness inherent in your soul, an impatience peeking out from my paper, and ever and always, the identity born of our drifting apart, our sacred, dead son. Look at how we move through the insipid liqueur of the afternoon now, or how I write on an infinitely reluctant iron machine, look at our whole life, from our adolescence with dogs and doorways, to this bitter, yellow, silent loneliness after summer has gone, a loneliness that fills us with inner passageways, with deserted labyrinths, with clothes that have fallen down. Neither you nor I. I don't know why I write, why I am writing you this letter, why I return to the bristling barbed-wire fence of language. We have not killed ourselves, and for that very reason we are dead, we are present at our absence, we pass again and again through the colorless hole of nothingness. We come in and we go out. We pass by doors and windows that do not concern us. No one as lonely as I am. No one as much a nobody as you. And now? We have stayed on here to be spectators of an afterlife of sky and summer that not a single living soul inhabits, watching the comet of death pass by, a bright trail of silent sea foam, until its very last moment as a comet, a season, water.

No, I swear to you. I write you this letter that I will bury among my papers so that you will never read it, doing violence to language so that the paper will become blank once again. I write you empty letters, from death to death, from no one to no one—what are we now?—to talk to you of everything that we have lost, and my words, my papers, keep falling into the vacuum of sun and time that is opening up between the two of us, like a well that touches the sky.

YOUR death, my son, has not darkened the world. It has been a dying of the light within light. The two of us here, deafened by tragedy, wounded by whiteness, mortally alive, telling you how it is.

Living on after myself, ill, I emerge each morning from a sleep that for all I know may be a fainting spell. My awakening bears a certain resemblance to a resurrection. It is almost like coming back to life. But it is a joyless resurrection, a return to life in order to cast an empty glance around me, in order to make sure that everything is in order—in disorder—and that I can go quietly back to dying again. Why even mention newspapers? I don't ask for the daily paper, I don't go out of my way to hunt one up, but if one chances to come my way, I glance through it the way one downs a laxative. What's going on in the world? The same things as always, naturally. The usual bloodshed and death, the same disgusting spectacle that humanity has presented since the beginning of time. The human situation is hopeless. Man is a mediocre creature and will never make anything of himself. France is testing its atomic bomb. People are terrified of atom bombs. Why? After so many centuries of bloodshed, wholesale butchery, cruelty, and dogged stubbornness, the most dignified thing mankind can do is commit collective suicide, on a global scale, and have done with it once and for all.

From the point of view of the ferromagnetic, from the point of view of the vegetative life on Mars, we would go out in a blaze of glory if we knew how to die at the right moment and all at the same time. Humanitarians inform us that every minute—or every second, I don't recall—a child dies somewhere. Children die of starvation, of course, and of sickness, poverty, abandonment, progress. They die of progress, because the world is making such tremendous progress that we now have precise statistics concerning children who die. What we don't have is the desire to feed them, although we keep careful records of how many of them die. With all the money that the bureaucratic apparatus for keeping close tabs on poverty costs, it might be possible to feed a few of those who are dying of starvation. But statistics are more important. First things first. We have not managed to wipe out poverty, nor have we ever really made any concerted effort to do so, but we have kept records on it, codified it, carefully checked into it, and explained it. That is progress.

So I set the daily papers aside in disgust and return to old familiar books, to authors who have played a more intimate and essential role in my life and accompanied me since my adolescence. Nothing new. Writers who, because I have reread them so often, seem as familiar to me as my own self. When I first began to read them, I wanted to be like them. Now I am in fact like them, and at times I even note things that are missing in their works and I put them in so they don't disappoint me as I read them. What difference does that make? That was what I wanted to be, that sort of writer. Nothing world-shaking, but since that was what I set out to do, my goal has been achieved.

And so I am again reading those who were my models, reading them on the way back from my intended destination, rather than on my way toward it, as in those days long since past, and today I feel what they felt: the tremendous frustration of having accomplished all one has set out to do, the emptiness of total fulfillment, what it is like to stand around with one's arms folded, doing nothing, even though one's arms appear to be moving about a great deal. This outward flailing about with one's arms—performing tasks, embracing, working, engaging in various activities, waving to people to say hello—masks an inner folding of one's arms, an idleness, a withdrawal from the world when one has already become inexorably withdrawn from one's self and is living one's life permanently on strike, refusing to lift a finger even though no one realizes it.

. . .

To all appearances I am busy doing things, even though I am really not doing anything at all. Out of a lack of desire, out of a lack of faith, out of a lack of everything, more or less. Not out of a lack of energy, naturally, or because my talents are failing me. I can still do my job. Language, my personal language, still possesses the resources to call man a miserable creature in a thousand different ways, to insult life in a thousand new turns of phrase. At this point I couldn't care less. A blank sheet of paper is much more beautiful than a sheet of paper covered with words. It took me a long time to discover this. Now I allow the blank sheet of paper to turn my life into a blank, and do nothing—except read books that I already know by heart, like things that have no savor left at all, try out medicines that are not going to cure me, piss out every last drop of my urine, say very little, remember things not worth remembering, and at times catch myself dreaming up plans for things I am going to write, for work I want to do, for garnering fame and glory, all of these being goals that I have long since achieved through my own efforts and left far behind me. They represent the force of inertia of the fight for recognition. One spends one's life doing battle, trying out certain things, and when one has tried everything and solved all the problems, one continues to scheme and plan, without realizing it. The inertia of success, let us call it. So why more books, more surprises, more travels, more photos, more ideological infighting, more risky ventures, and more politicking? I have now gotten to the place that I was determined to get to. In fact I have gotten nowhere, but I am satisfied nonetheless. I know that I don't have the talent to get any farther. Repeating myself may well prove to be detrimental. As for the world, it is quite obvious that I am not about to put it to rights, nor will others do so. The most honorable course would be to die in a guerrilla campaign, knowing that it too is utterly pointless. We have reached—I have reached and so has the world—the point where everything is so blindingly clear that it is unseemly to continue to cling to our illusions. We all know what is right and what the world would have to be like to be less despicable and less unjust. Confused ideologies or obscurantist theologies no longer stand as intermediaries between us and the world, as in the past. We are all face to face with the truth. Man exploits man—it is as simple as that. The innocent swaying back and forth of my invalid's rocking chair presupposes a tensing of the feeble muscles of thousands of badly undernourished men. If this were not the case the world would fall apart. Everything— from my humble convalescence to pleasure cruises on millionaires' yachts—is based on exploitation.

Injustice today has lost all of its pretended justifications and its traditional apologists. It is now perpetuated openly, as sheer injustice and nothing more. There is no longer any need for even the sketchy codices of human rights we once had. If this situation is not remedied it is because man simply feels no desire to do so.

What lazy, self-indulgent reluctance I feel, therefore, to become a part of this cynical and cruel world once again. Death and illness have removed me from it with the light touch of their dark hand. What self-indulgent reluctance to return to it. So I ask for another glass of milk, I open the old familiar book to the page I know best, I wander about the house like an old man in a home for the aged, I gaze upon the remains of summer with the eyes of someone who has somehow survived it, I sip my medicines, not quite knowing whether they are liqueurs of life or death, I write a bit, merely to test my muscular coordination, and am amazed that the typewriter answers me with a steady stream of gossipy chatter.

Neither alive nor dead, I read my classic authors, who tend to be Romantics, I listen to the dead with my eyes, as in the age of the Baroque, I spend my days in conversation with the dead, and I see my life as a novel of long ago: old-fashioned now and full of clichés, yet one I am still very fond of.

It has been a long time since I have written anything in this intimate journal, and I wonder now why I began it. That is what happens with every book, every work, every project I embark upon. The moment we interrupt our work, we question the nature of what we are doing. Why are we working, to what end? The ultimate raison d'être of a work in progress is its continuity. Once this continuity is broken, all other justifications become insufficient. Because it is not that every possible virtue and sacrifice on our part is required if work is to be well done; these virtues and sacrifices, rather, are born of such work, for it prompts them, awakens them, creates them. It is generally thought that a good writer produces a good novel. I believe equally that a good novel produces a good writer. One's wits are keener when one is working. The work in progress calls forth the best in us, stimulates us, heightens our sensibilities, improves us, exhausts us.

Hence by being interrupted, this book—like any other that is broken off—loses its ultimate meaning and reason for being, for it was neither immortality nor glory nor readers nor curiosity nor self-interest that motivated it. The ultimate reason behind this book is the discipline that it brings me, the continuity that it bestows on my life, since all of us are discontinuous.

What reason is there for writing an intimate journal? At this point and in my case, I am not writing a journal out of vanity, certainly, nor out of egocentricity, nor out of eagerness to be a literary celebrity, but rather in an effort to discover an ultimate simplicity, in order to escape from that artificiality that in the final analysis all literary genres presuppose. If one does not want novelistic tricks, poetic effects, the usual trumpery that the professional writer has at his disposal, to stand between the reader and himself, one can have recourse to the intimate journal, or write one's memoirs. But memoirs too are embellished by the mist of memory. The intimate journal, on the other hand, is immediate, the present moment at its most painful, confession that is not only sincere but urgently needed as well. What happens then—and this is the great lesson to be learned from keeping an intimate journal—is that we discover that we are no longer capable of simplicity, of being as we really are. Paradise is lost to us, we are corrupted by culture, it is impossible for us to make ourselves like unto a little child, and thus the intimate journal turns out to be full of lyrical turns of phrase, of purple prose, of highly contrived improvisations, or else, if one opts for a more direct prose style, one ends up sounding like a household account book, trivial, superficial, monotonous. Paradoxically, it thus turns out that Shakespeare confesses more about himself by way of his rhetorical flourishes, Baudelaire by way of his musical effects, Quevedo by way of his baroque conceits, than the keepers of deliberately "objective" journals. There is no such thing as a genre that is a direct reflection of reality. What would be most direct would be not to write at all.

This being so, I must resign myself to writing literature in my intimate journal, and resign myself to its turning out to be something like the poem in prose of several dark months in my life, or the novel of a bad novelist. We are caught fast in culture; we have lost all spontaneity, all naturalness. The press has recently carried accounts of children in Galicia who were devoured by dogs that had returned to the wild. These children were not the victims of wolves, as was first reported, but of dogs who had reverted to the wild state. This is precisely what ought to happen to man, what one would like to happen to oneself: to become something of a wild creature once again, to return to a more natural state. Without going so far, of course, as to devour children raw.

. . .

So, as I remain as aloof from the world as possible, the world comes to me in the guise of an impatient reporter, a curious girl student. My life has been spent running after things, and now, when I would like to be left in peace in my quiet, solitary retreat, things, life, the outside world, take on the intrusive form of somebody or other wanting an interview, of a go-getting journalist dropping by, hot for a feature story, trying to drag out of me, in the space of three-quarters of an hour, the secret of success, the formula for fame and renown, the keys of the writer's profession.

"How did you make it to the top, how are you staying there?"

Look, my boy, there are no formulas, no recipes. Learn, and use your wits. Be patient, but don't fail to lose your patience each and every day. Be at peace with yourself, but don't leave anyone else in peace. Or the stocky little girl student with glasses, smiling, an unconditional admirer of your work: "How does one write an article, how does one compose a novel?" They always ask these things. Do you go to bed early, are you a late riser? They think the secret lies in some vital formula, in getting up and working at the crack of dawn so that God will give them a hand—since they're fresh then—or in toiling far into the night so that the Devil will. They haven't the patience to wait and see what happens. They want to steal the secret from you in half an hour, leave with the formula and the alchemical knowledge required to manufacture gold at night, even though it's fool's gold or mere coin of the realm.

They don't know that it is all a question of endless patience, as the saying goes. But at the same time a sort of impatient patience. That even in the end there is no truth that one has in one's possession, but rather that one must search for the philosopher's stone all over again every day, and find it among the dull gray stones that are the commonest kind everywhere. Try to drink of the fountain of eternal youth, which may well come gurgling out of the kitchen faucet.

The interviewers, male and female, television networks, radio stations, newspapers. What do they want from a person? Nothing, obviously. It is just that one is a recognizable face, a cheeky character who will fill a space, take up a few minutes of air time, help bring in a few pesos. We have all done this and exploited the famous man, milking him of a little popularity and making a bit of cash out of him. One can say yes or no to these many requests, but what one cannot possibly do is believe that this is fame, that this is glory. Well, yes, come to think of it, this really is fame and glory. Pure shit.

They get the titles of all my books mixed up and the only thing they want is for me to repeat the same old hackneyed anecdotes about myself. Larra said that every anniversary is a mistake in date, and I maintain that all fame is a misinterpretation of the facts. What have I posed as in life? As a hippie, a dandy, a ragamuffin, a revolutionary, everything. That's what they want, for you to play your role. Like children, they keep wanting to hear the same story, the same fairy tale. There is a sort of intellectual anthropophagy, a cultural cannibalism, that has always been a source of concern to me. The masses do not devour books, songs, stories, or images. The masses devour living beings. Man is driven by a need to eat up man. The common horde goes to the movies not to follow a plot, but to devour a person, an actor or an actress. Books are not enough by themselves. It is the author who is of interest. He must be seen, touched, eaten alive. The thousands of paintings by Picasso are not enough by themselves. Picasso in his undershorts must be seen, touched, heard, read, listened to, devoured. Picasso was edible. He allowed himself to be thoroughly chewed before being swallowed. This is the secret. If you are not edible, digestible, nutritious, you may very well die of hunger. In order to eat of all this you must first let yourself be eaten. You must have a certain identifiable taste. "If I taste of anything, my taste will be for the earth to enjoy," Rimbaud said. Not so, as a matter of fact. Nowadays the taste that one has must be for the mass media, for the common horde to enjoy.

It has always been so, and circumstances today favor this tendency more than ever. Humanity has a thirst for humanity. Man, the adoring animal. We are driven by a need to adore another human being. Those who adore God also give him a human guise. Otherwise he would have no grace or charm. Intellectual anthropophagy is a fact, as are many other varieties. People look for a person behind politics, art, culture. It is impossible to do away with the cult of personality. Various socialist regimes have sought to do so, for very good reason and with very little success. Man is not made for abstractions. Man needs man. Humanity swallows up politicians, artists, heroes, geniuses, beautiful women.

That's why they come, to devour me from the feet up, since to a modest degree I am edible. If you are covered with glory you feed multitudes. If you enjoy only a modicum of popularity, as might be the case at a given moment in your career, you feed four starving journalists and four emaciated female university students. Humanity feeds upon itself. Neither landscape nor geography nor history is of the slightest interest unless we add human seasoning to it. Every landscape must be a landscape with human figures. This is because people need to believe in themselves. All of us here on earth are so lost, so devoid of the feeling that we have a destiny, humanity is at such loose ends that it needs the example of those who are great, those who are determined, those who have won fame and glory, those who appear to have a destiny, even though in fact they too have none.

So when they come to see me or take me somewhere so that I may be seen, I try to give them a feeling of security, of great security, since William Blake said that if the sun were to doubt for a single moment, it would no longer shine. What people want is precisely that: human suns, figures who are not assailed by doubts, beings who are certain of their destiny. That is how politicians and leaders of the masses triumph. Without going that far, the writer, for example, reassures people and radiates a feeling of security if he himself has such a feeling or gives the appearance of having it. What most fascinates this indecisive human horde is decisiveness, even if it is entirely feigned. An out-and-out lie is more convincing than a hesitant truth. I endeavor, along with Blake, never to doubt for a moment, like the sun, even though I really spend my life mooning.

Autumn. Asthenia. An empty sky, half-lights and half-deaths. Deaths and resurrections of each day, each hour. I don't feel well, but I couldn't care less; I am too well, considering I am merely a ghostly spectator of the world, a white face peeking over the walls of the cemetery of existence, looking inside, toward the corral of the dead, as someone once said in another context. Life? A continual, fierce ambush waiting for sex to come along, with furniture and offices in between, nothing else. Men and women look at each other out of the corner of their eye, spy on each other, hasten and postpone the moment of capture. Sex is a crime without a victim or with a victim. Baudelaire had a thing or two to say on the subject. There is a cruelty, an implicit vampirism, something grim and cynical in the battle between the sexes.

From shops to taxis, from the theater to the bedroom, from the depths of the shadows, from behind panes of glass, store windows, clothes, and parks, men and women seek each other out and misunderstand each other's moves in the cruel, monotonous, and eternal sexual crime game. Meanwhile, bridges span the sea or stairways rise and touch the vault of air overhead. The one thing that is certain is that the sexual sewer overflows and floods the world each night. A stinking zoological reality. In our shame at the baseness of all this, which is simply a dynamics of the herd, we have created lyricism, philosophy, complexity, metaphysics. As I have said repeatedly: all culture is simply man's desperate effort to dignify himself, to adorn himself with the trappings of transcendence. Religion wants to give us a soul, and culture wants to dress us up in a suit.

We are opaque and naked. Autumn. Asthenia. My head is so heavy that it is decapitating me all by itself. My arms are weighing me down with a ballast of shadows. My muscles are thickening with sleep. I am an empty garment fearfully treading the world's false vegetation, death's pitfall covered over with branches and leaves.

I have conversations with my dead son on department-store escalators. In front of newsstands I am a page ripped off, being blown away by the wind. Life has emptied itself of time now, and time has emptied itself of days. We create time by living, hoping, going on. If one resigns from life, time no longer exists. Time is our impatience. Without impatience, the spheres stop circling and the world reveals its inanity: a pointless joke, an old piece of worthless junk, a fallen thing.

When I hope for nothing, seek nothing, aspire to nothing, all that is left is the tedious, basic movement of life, its dull repeated mechanism. Time, that basic category and aura of all things, has been abolished. Yes, it is our impatience that creates time, as our loneliness creates God. The moment we no longer lend our assent to the great abstractions, they dissolve in thin air. Now that I have no desires left, time no longer exists: there are only seasonal variations in the weather. Perhaps not even the latter. For metaphysical *tiempo* and climatological *tiempo* are more inextricably intermingled than they appear to be.* It may well be that only climatological *tiempo* exists, what men who live in the span measured

* In Spanish, the word *tiempo* means both *time* and *weather*. [*Translator's note.*]

by calendars call the time or season of high-pressure areas and storms. We have made a metaphysical category out of time in the latter sense, by converting it into Time, with a capital *T*. Time without man is simply meteorology.

Time, autumn, asthenia. "You are suffering from asthenia," the doctor tells me. I think it is the world that is suffering from asthenia. I shut myself up in the house to make the return trip to the past. When time doesn't exist, it isn't even necessary to journey in space. The past is right here, and hence it is possible that I may write a book on my childhood, another book on my childhood, which may or may not be a novel—what does it matter?—since at this point my childhood is neither a literary evocation of the past nor a poem, but rather an ordinary occurrence, something that is happening to me every day.

In my childhood I am my own son. That son too will be lost someday, like all the others, but right now he is very much alive for me. The child I have lost is the child I once was. One is one's own father. That orphan of my early years, that child I once was, now has a father: me. I keep confusing this dead child with that other dead child, because they are the same child, and no matter which of the two I am writing about, I am writing about the child, about the essential nucleus of childhood that makes me what I am, about the tender golden primal ooze that I was, that I am, that I have been, that I continue to be this very minute, that I will be. "Homer is young each morning and yesterday's newspaper is already terribly old," Charles Péguy tells us. Homer told us things. He endeavored to tell of the childhood of humanity, or the childhood of culture at any rate. The child, that child, this child, my child, every last child down through the ages—all children are the same child, just as the rose is all roses—is new each morning, but my self of this very moment is already terribly old. In this asthenic autumn, in this autumnal asthenia, the idea of that book tugs at me: a profound, prolonged immersion in childhood, in the primordial past, in something that is as fresh as early morning within the self, whereas the self of this instant is terribly remote, dead and deeply buried.

I scrape off my beard with the razor to see whether that will rejuvenate me a little, but it's not a good idea to shave corpses because it makes them look worse.

ARTICLES, articles, articles. A form of self-destruction. I have gone back to writing articles. Hundreds, thousands of articles. In the beginning they were my way of gradually creating a self, a construct built up stone by stone, step by step, making a name, a man, and a life day by day, word by word. Today, now that everything is ended, they are a self-destruction, and with each article I remove one of the supports of my life, of my *oeuvre,* dismantling piece by piece the useless framework of my life that I have so laboriously put together. Critics, readers, people in general say that the writer runs the risk of burning himself out by turning out so many articles, but what the writer—contrite, numb from the cold, alone, ailing, devoid of everything—wants, more than anything else, is precisely that, and has discovered in the article a way of going up in flames, of disappearing, a pointless, fragmentary sort of work wherein he can strip himself bare, page by page, as a tree sheds its leaves one by one, and die. Articles were my battle-axe, my stiletto, the weapon that life gave me in order to sack and pillage, the trusty short-bladed sword with which to conquer and build a little personal empire. And now I am turning this weapon against myself, I am hacking my life's work up into articles, I am spreading myself thin, I am fragmenting myself, for to write books is to construct with the desire to build something that will endure, with architectonic faith, and this now strikes me as a perverse endeavor. I have written a few books, not many, but too many nonetheless. I shall perhaps write a few more, attracted by the vertigo of utter uselessness, by that concentrated emptiness that a book represents. What I would prefer is this suicide in the form of article writing. Since I have not had the courage to destroy myself, I am setting about to destroy my lifework, to chop up what could have been a complete, solidly built whole into scattered articles. With each article I write I lose the possibility of writing a poem, an essay, a story, something more coherent and more lasting. Hence in each article I lay out in a shroud and bury forever a direction of my life, or several directions, thus leaving the whole incomplete, merely hinted at superficially, broken off, broken up, mistreated, miscarried.

I am arriving, I readily confess, at that negative sensual gratification afforded by the newspaper or magazine article offered up as a form of sacrifice, as an immolation, as the laying out for burial of children that might otherwise have every chance of living and growing. With each article I undo a knot in the warp and woof of my existence, and I am thereby becoming looser and looser, lighter and lighter, devoid of possibilities, unfulfilled.

Overcome with fear, drenched with sweat and trembling with chills or fever, with a profound sense of insecurity, with rage, with the light of understanding or without, I write articles every day, thereby undoing my entire *oeuvre,* and I contemplate that splendid mirror that I was once able to contrive, shattered now into a thousand shards of articles, a mirror doomed to remain henceforth nothing but broken bits and pieces. What I want now is not to create a lifework, but to destroy it. I rip articles out of myself the way a person might claw off great strips of his skin, the way the leper sees great shreds of his flesh falling off. I have discovered that the article is a brilliant way of turning into an utter failure.

I have found only one truth in life, my son, and that was you. I have found only one truth in life and I have lost it. I go on living by weeping for you in the night with tears that sear the darkness. Little fair-haired soldier who ruled the world, I have lost you forever. Your eyes made the blue of the sky a solid thing. Your hair gave the very day a golden glow. What remains now that you are gone, my son, is a fickle, totally capricious universe (thus resembling what the ancients tell us of the nature of Jupiter), a sickeningly vague jumble of summers and winters, a promiscuity of sun and sex, of time and death, through all of which I wander aimlessly only because I haven't the least idea what one must do in order to have done with living and get on with dying. If I knew, I would do that and only that.

How stupid the day is, and the fullness thereof. Who is deluded by this blue sky, this midday full of laughter? Who is supposed to be taken in by this immense lie of sun-drenched months and green fields? Why this vain prowling on the part of death along the coasts of spring? The sun is sordid and the day glows with sheer gratuity, is radiant with pure emptiness, and in the nodding of the world's head in a banal breeze all I see is the vegetable stubbornness of life, its stupidity of a blind plant. It is persistence that forever rules the universe, never intelligence. Its one and only law is mere persistence. Boredom alone moves the clouds in the sky and the waves in the sea.

HERE we are, my son, your mother and I, amid folding screens, amid kitchens without a spark of life or color, amid advertisements, fine print, and medicines: so lonely, so far apart, with nothing to bring us together, and the universe, my son, the universe that your capital letters organized around you, a universe that is now like the scattered debris of a shipwreck. By murdering you, life has killed itself; it has lost all meaning and is paying for its crime in sunny afternoons that nobody believes in and nightfalls shrouded in fog when no one is happy.

I write mechanically, my son, and glimpse in the east what I don't wish to see, sacred ashes that the sun takes no notice of each morning, and I think of the color of your hair, the texture of your eyes, the new outline of your little heart, which were the result of thousands of generations, the fortunate, successful outcome of the species, a credit to human raw material, that has failed yet again and revealed the irreversible condition of our blood, doomed to decline and fall as surely as autumn leaves. During the long hours of the night, my son, I cough, I spit, I weep, I tremble, I organize, wide awake, the nightmares that sleep immediately disorganizes, and I count on you to still be there when dawn comes.

I am the one and only corpse in all of history that has ever written a book, and in the world is a trail of women dying for their sex, and a taste of wine that no one savors anymore, and with its attack on you the world has lost its last chance of having any meaning and any right to the stars that shine each night. So the pyramid in my soul keeps growing: the sacred space, the crypt that I have you buried in inside me, between two ribs, between my epigastrium and feeling, and I see myself in the mirrors of department stores and it is only an image in a mirror because you are living in the womb that has been born in me for you.

A time of decadence is at hand, everything is posthumous, life has now gone on too long and politicians carry out their betrayals each morning in a halfhearted, clumsy way, for the bird on the branch and the clock in the tower are merely awaiting the final collapse, the last sigh of the galaxy that will free all of us of the laws of heredity and return us to relativity and nothingness.

We go on sad and gloomy excursions through ancient cities, we utter your name as if you were somewhere far away, we string ourselves on a thread of red or white voices asking questions about eternity, and from time to time I take refuge in a windowpane, in that space of doubt that exists between the glass and reality, so as to take communion in your flesh. Children's straw-bottomed chairs, grave rocking chairs, steeds with sky-blue manes ask me about you, ask each other about you, and as you doubtless know, we climb to the top floors of houses under construction and look down from there on this moment in the late afternoon, with its smoke and time, that moment when it is conceivable that you might turn into a vulgar plaster statue or a distant light before our eyes.

TOILETS, public restrooms, lavatories, those dark, empty, echoing blue places where I take refuge and take on my coppery texture once again, a special attraction to those sordid places, with light coming from a courtyard outside, where the woman has experienced in terror the twofold metamorphosis of her body into a wolverine and a statue, where the man has witnessed in shame the growth of a sparse, sick jungle amid the roots of his civic glory.

Toilets, public restrooms, lavatories, the underside of a house, the underside of a life, the underside of the world, washrooms, all the inane, ugly words that have been used to utter the unutterable, with double grapes and a wet white corpse in the bottom of the bathtub. I take refuge in toilets as if I intended to die there, since in the rest of the house or the hotel there is a frozen dignity of suit cloth and carved beams with a solidity that inspires respect, but there in the toilet, amid its pale, putrid mirrors, the pink bodies of children, the fat-assed souls of women are still moving, and I understand more clearly there that the only truth is the light from the window overlooking the courtyard, a gray light that fosters no illusions, that has neither the twilight artifice of the sun nor the fake-jewelry moral brilliance of the night.

Toilets, public restrooms, lavatories, water closets, washrooms, men's rooms and ladies' rooms, bathrooms, pink pants and esparto-grass scrub brushes that the ocher fruit of our life sticks to, the lusterless cement of our being, and that smell of innocence and uremia that is the sum and substance of our soul and the only thing that will remain of us when we die, even though we have been authors of treatises and builders of dikes. The city is a prostituted piano burned to a cinder that only I knew how to play. I flee from it and hate it now. The country is a pastoral instrument, something illiterate and irritating, and literature no longer pulls the wool over anyone's eyes. You believed in women, and then one day you discovered their reverse side made up of toilets and mirrors, of powder boxes and waste products. In the blank mirror of the toilet you gaze at the empty space where your conscience ought to be and play your soul like a musical instrument. Only the mirror in the toilet knows the story of your life and how little sun there is left in it. There is a bird of cold pecking at the window and a sky-blue horse looking at me like a child. Explosions of red and light set off a bonfire around me and the clock of my pleura hurts like a secret. Winter is laying siege to me with its ailing troops, as prose flows beneath the pillow. But I am destined to take medicines and tell the dead the news of the day. Mild illnesses repair to my body as migratory birds repair to the trunk of night, I am a dismal sewer of sorrows and sicknesses, and I weep tears for your tiny absence till Sunday.

I will die writing illegible pages, because the man who is dead inside me is getting bigger and bigger; he is like a sad friend, and rummages aimlessly and listlessly through my belongings. This is what living is, this is what dying is (I don't remember if I took my medicine at the time I was supposed to), this is what it's like to go about with half of one's self a shadow, ashes, growing denser and more respectable with each passing day. Death does not exist. Only the dead man exists. The dead man is alive, he arrives like an intruder, pays a call on us, and suddenly I catch myself acting like a dead man, with the gestures, the lapses of memory, the acts of self-denial of someone who has passed away. I know this and often think about it. "This is the dead man's doing," I say to myself when my belly weeps, when I leave a sheet of paper I've been writing on behind on a rooftop, when I think of a woman I have known as if she were an instrument or a tool. This is the dead man's doing. The dead man is gradually taking possession of my life, the dead man that I shall be and that I am already becoming little by little, as when one is given a new post, job, position, and is surprised at oneself and splits in two. When the dead man has taken possession of all your things, even though he really has no need of them and no illusions about them but nonetheless covets them, you die.

Earlier in life, the dead man wasn't even noticeable. They say that a man is many men, that his psyche splits into several different personalities. Freud speaks of three such personalities: the ego, the id, and the superego, or something of that sort. It seems to me that there are two of each of us: the one who's alive and the one who's dead. The dead man doesn't make his presence felt until a certain age. He appears one day, when we have fallen ill or received a visit of condolence, and stays on forever after. We think he's gone away, like a friend dressed in mourning who's paid us a call, but he comes back. I know now that he will never leave for good. Earlier on, the dead man was around off and on. Today he lives with me like a tenant to whom I have sublet part of myself. The dead man that I am, that I shall be. "Must be stable gentleman," the ads for rooms to let specify. Well, the dead man is a stable gentleman who has stayed on to live in my inside rooms. I do a great deal of writing in order to get away from him, for the only thing I have not yet taught my dead man to do is write. I don't think he'll ever learn. The dead man doesn't like me to write. The dead man likes us to go look at apartments that we have no intention of renting, to visit the doctor's office, provided we do so without hope, to wear the clothes of three winters ago that we loathe. The dead man, my dead man, doesn't like going to the movies or seeing me sit down to write. He thinks I'm going to get away from him by writing, as if my typewriter were a fast racing car or a bicycle. To tell the truth, I write as if I were pedaling furiously, forever fleeing from something.

One gets used to living with one's corpse. Admittedly, it is an uncomfortable situation, but a person can get used to anything. Well, you think, it would be worse to be hunchbacked or have some troublesome disease. But as it turns out, matters don't end there. When you have introduced the corpse to your friends, when you take it everywhere with you, like a relative who embarrasses you, when everyone has tumbled to the fact that you are you and your dead man, that you are your dead half and your live half, you one day discover, in a toilet or a taxi, that all that is left of you is the dead man, that the dead man has taken your place, and you are overcome with horror, since you are no longer a live person putting up with a dead person, cohabiting with him, but a dead man who only remembers the live one.

In any event, the dead man and I have now perhaps entered a period of stable relations, like a bored, dull-witted couple who are going to remain hopelessly married forever. When I can't find a handkerchief, when I don't wear the shirt I'd really like to, when I pick up a book that doesn't interest me, I say: "This is the dead man's doing." The dead man is gradually taking over my life, and the idiot doesn't realize that by doing me in he is doing both of us in.

A Sunday drains away like a dying sea beyond hope of recovery. If I pick up the telephone, I'm afraid they'll connect me with the cemetery. The cold shrouds me in strips of fever and I return from my travels posthaste and posthumously. I have lived such a long life that I can put my hand in any pocket and take out a baby tooth that I lost at a very tender age. I was once a wrathful statue that defied constellations, and now my body is a home for the aged where a host of oldsters yearn to smell a rose. All I have left is my head, like a high window, to drink in the sky and bite into some unknown apple.

SHE has gotten up early, feeling restive, impelled by a secret, by a tiny happiness—how pitiful her craftiness is—and has moved about the house more vivaciously, as in the days when you were still alive, having brought home two red roses, two flowers sheathed in green, the key to her secret, the center of her tender little conspiracy, because there had to be something, my son, and the two roses were there, the warm glow of a long-gone happiness in the gray of the house.

Yes, it was as though she had gone to the farthest limits of our happiness, to the very bottom of days, to the bas-relief of memory, there where you still laugh amid golden seashells, to cut those two flowers—though in fact they came from the street market—so that the light of a time when we were happy would catch fire for the last time in this house. In the afternoon—listen closely—we were silent as sleepwalkers in the back seat of a car, hurrying out to the sad, distant, empty hole in the ground, and the autumn was red, gold, slow, thick, as if you were still alive, and we passed through so many shady groves, my son, such a denseness of dead people, so much light piled up on the edges of the afternoon, before plunging into the nonexistent blue tunnel in which you are not waiting for us, and we took the two roses with us, like a summons to your blood, a call from red to red, from life to life, from life to—oh, alas, alas—death.

THE cold, my son, the cold, the chill companion of a poverty-stricken childhood, a filthy scratching cat that was my only friend for so many years, the cold, whose ivy has been creeping more and more luxuriantly through my wintery body my whole life long, and now that still deeper shadow has overtaken me, it grips me by the throat with a sad, stubborn singleness of purpose, or sings in my bronchial tubes with the dark metallic overtones of night, or cinches my belly in tightly, cutting through it like an invisible sharp sword edge, like a freezing-cold fishing knife, till it leaves me doubled over, shrinking with fear, defenseless. Heavy cumbersome garments, fires, stoves, sources of heat in which I clothe my loneliness, and the cold inside me, like a great urn full of poison, like the barren, desolate, inhospitable center of my self.

Cold is more than cold, cold is the enmity life harbors against me, the hostile face it makes at me, an attack on me that it has launched repeatedly through the years, a crystal serpent, an ice-cold bonfire that consumes me. I take things to ward off the cold, hot drinks, medicines in the middle of the afternoon, but I note how the cold is little by little taking the place of my soul, how gradually the one and only thing my conscious mind is aware of is cold, nothing but cold. It is not that I am getting colder inside, but that my vitals are coldness itself, and my heart an iceberg that is becoming a heavier and heavier weight than I should by right be asked to bear. That is what going on living must be, my son, a passing from sunlight to shadow, from heat to cold, from summer to winter, a winter that we spend more and more of the year in now, with a long sojourn in the month of November that we once believed was a transitory phenomenon and is now becoming permanent. Cold was once a visitor dropping by to pay a call. Today it arrives for a long, long stay, or worse still, I myself am that cold. Once upon a time I passed through the month of November as if it were a transfer point between one season and another. Today I see myself fated to live forever in cold seasons as chilly as train stations. The cold is becoming my way of experiencing time, my most metaphysical personal experience, my one interchange with what is other than myself.

Cold is in the streets outside as well, a fog of unreality, or that sun blown hither and thither in a north wind, the wind of my childhood, the light-flooded desolation that met my eyes on those long-ago mornings when I used to go out into the streets at a very early hour. This is precisely what greets me now. I should like to explain to you what you no longer see, my son, what no longer sees you, I should like to explain the light of this autumn to you, or the wild smell of this cold wind, everything that would have been the structure of the present if you were here, and that without you does not even exist; it is merely an unwelcome, insistent allusion to things already experienced, things that belong forever to the past now. In the half-shadow of the world, in the kingdom of cold, I light up little circles of your life, that school with sun and shadow that you attended for a brief period, that afternoon in March when you were a child among other children and I was afraid that I would lose you in their midst, that afternoon when I was overcome with anxiety on realizing that your voice, your cries, could easily be confused with other voices, other cries. A child indistinguishable from the wild forest of childhood. Today I could illuminate so many instants of your life—of your life?—but I am terrified by the heart's vertigo, the unfathomable depths of memory, the unbounded power of grief, and I find myself unable to reach out and touch the golden, sacred flesh of your memory and instead remain on the lukewarm perimeter, glimpsing a school with a garden, or an early-morning song, or rose-colored, talkative animals, all the sweet metamorphoses that the world was able to conjure up for you.

Exiled from your kingdom of light and speech, I wander from one cold country to another, and I will forever remain the exile now, the man who passes by, in the afternoon, with the collar of his overcoat turned up, gazing at lights and shop windows, because you have taken off somewhere and left me outside, because only you aimed at the warm center of life and hit it, and I never shall, and I am painfully aware that I am an expatriate, and everything I pass is only the outskirts of a city, an outlying district, excluded from the golden secret of the world. I have told someone that you were the only truth I have ever encountered. You were, you are, the only truth I find within myself. Your memory, that photograph in which you look at me with grave eyes over the wide-brimmed breakfast cup, are the only things I have left to keep me from being worthless in my own eyes.

This book, my son, that was born heaven only knows how, that unwittingly grew around you, has become the secret place where the two of us meet, the one refuge of my conversation, of my monologue with you, even though this monologue is my whole life now and you and I do nothing but talk together these days, without anyone overhearing us. The other afternoon I saw a little pig, a suckling pig, hanging by its snout at the door of a butcher shop, with its tail still curled in a delightful, amusing corkscrew. What a conversation you and I would have had with this creature. It is your soul now that hangs innocently from a cold hook. If you were not a child I would read you a passage that I have just come across in a book: "We are all in the depths of a hell each moment of which is a miracle." A miserable miracle, I would add. The universe has no plot save cruelty nor any logic save stupidity. In the dark gardens of cold, a child suddenly looks at me, his eyes slowly meet mine, and with a shudder of horror I discover, my son, that it is you who look at me from the depths of the eyes of all children.

❡ 176

You are not you, you are not simply yourself, but the depths all children have in common. The dark, clear waters of childhood flow past full of innocent eyes, a series of eyes opening wide, one after the other, those of the timid child, the happy child, the sad child, the hostile child, the unknown child, the girl child, and at the end of this series your eyes gaze at me, as from the bottom of a deep, limpid river. It is only in a child's gaze that you suddenly come a little closer to me, from the depths to the surface, but my hand trembles when I touch this child, I drown in the knowledge that you are alive and yet not alive, I fearfully breathe in that child's wild woodland scent, the scent of childhood itself, terrified in the face of the fact that you are at once alive and not alive.

I flee forever the warm continent, the cries of children, that secret garden that still, alas, gives forth the fragrance that is you, because you are not you, and I prefer the image of you, sacred and intact, to the confusion of gentle little lambs. How far inside the cold you have left me, how lost my big hand is in the vagueness of the world without the tiny firmness of your hand. How cold, my son, the silent, empty, desolate corner with your toys is on this cold morning.

She was silent, there in the center of a tragic summer, with a momentary gleam of fear in her eyes, suddenly alight with time and news, come from a far-off afternoon that was a fiasco, liberated from dark pieces of furniture, a sphinx become an adolescent once again, fed by springs of memory engulfed in shadow, freed of something, I don't know what, saved from that other woman whose face remained in profile, backlighted, standing out sharply against all the rocks. And she was wearing a shirt open at the neck, a pair of pants that were threadbare from being repeatedly brushed by the wings of that black summer, the splendor of the liquors of the present striking her eyes full of quiet terror, of motionless drama, of oblique light, a dark adolescent altar lamp in the July light. Then I lost her again, as on painful Sundays, till the speed of colors brought her back to me and we found ourselves in one of those enormous coffeehouses with vast expanses of empty space like a railway station and women growing sadder and sadder as the afternoon wore on. Holding her child's hand I fell into schools whose meaning was indecipherable, I visited halls where all hope was lost, I traversed unwanted gardens. Holding her big child's hand I went down streets that were foundering in a humble dry fire, and we visited unstable shops in which a time made of mud swelled like the outsize varnished belly of the most sincere vessels, until I was reborn in black taverns with corridors of wine, in the back room of which a bullfighter was dying at the dubious hour when those blinded by barium opened their eyes to the miracle of blood. We said age-old words and then I put my hand on her hair as on the silent flight of a bird without memory, and I lighted her dark fire by awakening the sorrow of her cheeks. We met, later on, in public squares as crowded as life, in parks reread by the sun, and all the blackness of time had accumulated in her hair, all the drama of age in her eyes. A bold puppy's nose, the mouth of a greedy child, the hands of a boy, breasts that I divined were solid with shadow, thighs as glorious as battles, something of the black-pelted female wolf cub about her, and always the dark welling up of her life, flowing into her flesh like a fire.

My son, one day I saw a duck in the water. I would have liked to tell you about it. It was a sunny day, we were in the country, and there the duck was, in the sun, in the water. It was white and not very big, you know? Just that, my son. I know that it is important to you. To me, too. I am writing to you, my son, from another death that is not yours. From my death. Because the thing that distresses me most is that you and I will not meet even in death. Each one of us remains in his own death, forever. Death is distance, nothing but distance. Now you can live only through me, insofar as you were part of my life, my son. I can live only through you. The only part of me that is alive is the part of you that is alive: memory. Now that you are dead, all the talkativeness of the world speaks to me in your silence. All the silence of the world speaks eternally in your adorable talkativeness. Such an oral creature, possessed of such a gift for speech, cannot be silent forever. Your prodigious capacity for expressing things, for naming them, everything you would have said continues to be said all by itself, without you, but it takes on the flower shape of your mouth.

So you go on talking to me forever, and this book never closes, but remains eternally open between you and me, because we go on talking together night and day, and the substance of my life is simply this dialogue. If you only knew, my son, from what wasteland I am writing to you, from what a muddle of tears and clothes strewn about everywhere, from what confusion and apathy. I am living death, because one must live death in life, for then there is no death in death. Sleepless, grieving, worn out, cowardly, all alone, ill, heart-wounded, I am here among your things, my son, neither alive nor dead, unable to make up my mind which of the lonely spots that await me I should go to, hesitant amid so many absences, horrified by the sun that has come out today, a sun that means nothing and is only a tremendous obstacle between you and me.

I am about to bring this journal to a close, this journal that continues to be eternally open, the first one I wrote about the child who was a babe in arms then: promise, torrent, possibility, total life, sacred flesh, my son:

Putting the baby to sleep, the baby in my arms, the moment I come home, late, just in time to put the baby to sleep. "He was already falling asleep; you're late getting home." The street, the frantic pace, cars, buses, the office. Putting the baby to sleep in the rocking chair, sleep, sleep, my baby, sleep. The rocking chair moving back and forth, back and forth in the dark, wood on wood, the rocking chair in the shadow, with soft upholstered arms and the swaying of the wood back and forth on the parquet floor, like a sleigh, like a boat in the water. Sleep, my baby, sleep. People, the smell of the office on my hands, the street signs, the scars of smoke and ashes, hands hardened by other hands, hands inured to money, the exchange of greetings, buying-and-selling contracts, telephones, typing. The fast pace of transactions, the wound of telephones ringing constantly, the street. At last this quiet rocking to and fro, with everything in perfect balance, this shadowed oasis of home, this swaying back and forth of the rocking chair, with the baby in my arms, as darkness falls. You've gotten home just in time to put him to sleep.

There, there. Sleep, my baby, sleep. Sleepmybabysleep. The rocking chair. We had to buy the rocking chair one day, or perhaps it was a whim, I don't remember, as we went down that street, dark streets, nightfall, dusty shops, the rocking chair in the window, upholstered in green cretonne, with a colored stripe running down the center from top to bottom, soft stuffed arms with fringe, nice short fringe, and semicircular rocker feet, like the springs of a coach, like the runners of a sleigh. The rocking chair. "Oh, look, what a pretty rocking chair!" That sad afternoon when we went out shopping together, with an enthusiasm born perhaps that morning that we kept up by an act of will throughout the day, as it began to pall on us, ceasing to be enthusiasm and without our realizing it turning into a specific purpose, no longer an enthusiasm but a definite plan, something that had to be done, and then no longer even a purpose, but an unpleasant task, a tradition, a routine, a monomania, a vague necessity, who knows what.

Going out shopping. In the morning it was a joyous plan for the day. In the afternoon, a vague duty. By nightfall, still out shopping, all the disconcerting confusion of one's entire life. Buying a rocking chair: why a rocking chair, what for? To take naps in, on afternoons when there's time for a nap, for quiet afternoons sitting outdoors in a rocking chair, rocking the air, rocking the world. To sit in in the morning, on mornings of leisure, out in the sun and the shade, reading the newspaper. The rocking chair moving to and fro. The rocking chair rocking life and love, and solitude and company. Its movement, the fun of it making life seem less important and things in general less serious.

There aren't any mornings of leisure, or afternoons with time for a nap. Ah yes, there are Sunday mornings. Sunday morning, when one is sleepy and has a headache and feels generally brutish after Saturday night's dinner. Sunday morning is for reflecting on the failure of life, for seeing the week from the reverse side, for seeing oneself in a luminous pause, coming from the dark stairways of work, habit, reconciliations. The afternoons with time for a nap, which are afternoons of frustrated desire, of reading in fits and starts, of silent, swollen lust, with no future, or only one future, and that one painful and unwanted. The rocking chair. Rocking in the rocking chair, imparting a false lightness to life, a back-and-forth movement that deludes us into thinking that things are going well, that all our problems can be resolved over a few drinks, with the same industrial optimism whereby a refrigerator produces cold. With the light fading, just as the shop was about to close, there on the long, steep street, they bought the rocking chair.

The salesman wasn't expecting to make that rather important sale at the last moment. What strange people customers are. There it was, between the darkness of the shop and the darkness of the street: the summer rocking chair, comfortable and light, with its joyful movement to and fro and its cretonne.

Once taken home, the rocking chair ran permanently aground, with no tide to float it off, bored, stranded in the gray sands of the household. It was just one more piece of furniture, one more place to sit, a chair with the soul of a boat that had never sailed between the sun and the shade of happy mornings, of summer afternoons. Until the baby was born.

Sleep, my baby, sleep.

The street, the cars, the steering wheel, the bus, the briefcase, the telephone, the contracts, the typewriter, the hectic pace, the silent, clumsy, daily flight of documents. Till the return home at night, the half-shadow, the baby in my arms, held against my chest, his head on my shoulder, a sweet-smelling armful, a weightless weight, petal-hands, a bundle radiating heat. Then the rocking chair began to make sense and have a future. One day they happened to put the baby in his arms, and he happened to sit down in the rocking chair with the baby. Simple acts linked together by the immanent logic of basic things. Sleep, my baby, sleep. Off to sleep, my boy, there you go. Sleepbabysleep.

The baby stirs slightly, speaks in bird-phrases, falls half asleep, keeps his eyes open in the dark, turned toward the painful light of the street, with gentle stubbornness. The light slowly dies in the baby's eyes. The baby's eyes, more wide-open than at any other time during the entire day, beam forth their greatest light before they close. The human voice in the baby's throat returns to its original state, a gurgle. The father's vague humming, the sound of the rocking chair sailing along, the sun-drenched voice of the baby uttering words that are mere sounds, sentences without words, syllables no ear has ever heard before. Sleep, my baby, sleep.

The baby's words are lost in the darkness, like the forgotten little round white pebbles that he has played with. The father's voice and the sea-surge of the rocking chair gradually become slower, deeper, more nocturnal. Every so often there is a burst of activity, a sudden acceleration, a joyous awakening on the part of the child, as though it were already morning after a minuscule night. The sound of the sea, the voyage, the jabbering in his sleep begin again. Sleep, my baby, sleep. The avid office, the hostile outside world, the stuffy house all fade into a blur, everything is far away now, forgotten in the rocking-chair voyage.

The dark voice and the clear voice move farther and farther off, covering great distances, passing through zones of light and shadow. The clear voice dots the vast dark field of the other voice with little grace notes of sound spaced farther and farther apart, becoming softer and softer. Peace was not to be found in the leather chair of the company manager nor in the spacious and hungry bed of another woman, nor in the resigned bed of every day, nor in the frenetic summers, nor in the restless sea, nor in the stabbing sun of hasty flight. One journeys toward peace in an unknown rocking chair that little by little takes on the form of a family. Without dreams, without hope, without struggle, without hunger, without sleep. The journey is the same with a child in one's arms, the journey toward one's son's sleep, with the briefcase full of paperwork still standing on the floor next to the rocking chair. It is a brief journey that will end when the baby has fallen fast asleep and is put into his cradle, with the last musical word, which has no letters, trembling on his lips. Sleep, my baby, sleep. After that one returns to gestures, memory, the usual reproaches ("but-of-course-that's-the-only-way-you-know-how-to-behave"), the dreary, minimal ceremony of dinner.

The journey goes on still; it is a simple blanking out of memory. An innocent and selfless rocking back and forth. Look what a lot of good we've gotten out of the rocking chair. Peace wasn't come by through reading books. Peace was journeying in a rocking chair, with a baby astride you who talks in his sleep. In the swaying back and forth of a rocking chair a life, a failure, a resignation, a distance, a fear, a loneliness, a cowardice, a love are being traced out. What a sweet, unsuspected way of giving up. Sleep, my baby, sleep. The rocking chair is made for giving up, for making the world and oneself smaller, for reducing everything to the brief and repeated journey back and forth, forth and back. The rocking chair is a piece of furniture for giving up.

Sleep, my baby, sleep. A sweet, magic piece of furniture. A hypnotic piece of furniture with undreamed-of powers. Who would ever have thought so when we bought the rocking chair? The surrender of self comes, full of sweetness, and the baby, once asleep, gives off all his perfume. These have been a few moments spent journeying and escaping. All the impossible gratitude for life—sleep, my baby, sleep—in the clear, indecipherable voice rocked gently to and fro.